THE AI EFFECT

Published by Spines
ISBN: 979-8-89569-738-2

THE AI EFFECT

How Technology is Enhancing My
Everyday Life!

T.C. Catz

Contents

DEDICATION

To those who dare to embrace the future of finance, those who seek knowledge and empower themselves with technology. May this book serve as a guide on your path to financial freedom and success in the age of artificial intelligence.

Preface

In an era defined by rapid technological advancements, the financial landscape is undergoing a profound transformation. Artificial intelligence (AI) is no longer a futuristic concept; it is a powerful force reshaping the way we invest, manage our finances, and plan for the future. This book aims to demystify the world of AI in finance and empower individuals to harness its potential for personal wealth creation.

We stand at a pivotal juncture where the intersection of technology and finance holds immense promise. AI offers unparalleled opportunities to streamline investment processes, enhance decision-making, and democratize access to financial services. However, navigating this uncharted territory requires a clear understanding of the tools, strategies, and ethical considerations involved.

This book serves as a comprehensive guide, providing both theoretical knowledge and practical insights into the world of AI-driven personal finance. It is designed for individuals of all financial backgrounds, from beginners seeking to enter the investment world to seasoned investors looking to refine their approach.

We invite you to embark on this journey of discovery, where you will explore the latest advancements in AI-powered financial technologies, learn how to leverage these tools effectively, and gain the knowledge and confidence to make informed investment decisions that align with your financial goals.

Introduction

To the curious minds, the tireless innovators, and the visionaries who strive to harness the boundless potential of AI for the betterment of all. We believe that understanding AI is not just for scientists and engineers; it's for everyone. We've meticulously researched, developed relevant topics, and crafted a manuscript that is both informative and enjoyable to read.

AI is an ever-evolving field, and the journey of understanding it is a lifelong endeavor. May this journey into the world of artificial intelligence inspire you to explore its possibilities, embrace its challenges, and shape its path for the benefit of our world.

It's a reality woven into the fabric of our daily lives, from the personalized recommendations we receive online to the voice assistants that respond to our commands. We'll explore the fundamentals of AI, its historical roots, its different types, and its applications in various sectors.

Rather, it's a guide for anyone who wants to understand the

basics of AI, its impact on society, and its potential to transform our world.

Book Cover_Mock-up

Why The N.E.R.D.Y. Way?

The **N.E.R.D.Y.** Way, a potent acronym that stands for kNowledge, **E**ducation, **R**esource, **D**iscovery for **Y**ou, embodies the spirit of this book. It's not just a journey through the world of AI; it's an invitation to embark on a lifelong adventure of learning, exploration, and constant evolution. As the field of AI progresses at an astonishing pace, so too must our understanding and engagement with it. The NERDY Way encourages you to embrace this dynamic and ever-changing landscape as a catalyst for personal growth and societal advancement.

Think of it as an ongoing dialogue, a conversation between you and the world of AI, where curiosity is your compass and exploration is your guide. This journey is not about reaching a destination; it's about the continuous process of learning, adapting, and evolving alongside the ever-expanding frontiers of AI. Embrace the challenges and opportunities that come with this journey, for within them lies the potential to unlock your own capabilities and contribute to a future where technology empowers humanity.

The N.E.R.D.Y. Way is a mindset, a philosophy that encourages you to approach AI with a sense of wonder and a spirit of inquiry. It's about recognizing the profound impact AI is having on every aspect of our lives and acknowledging its potential to reshape our world. This mindset fosters a deep appreciation for the transformative power of AI while also recognizing the critical need for responsible development and deployment. It's about understanding the intricate workings of AI systems, their strengths, and limitations, and using this knowledge to make informed decisions about their use.

The N.E.R.D.Y. Way isn't just about acquiring knowledge; it's about applying it to create a better future. This journey is about using your understanding of AI to solve global challenges, foster collaboration between humans and machines, and shape a future where technology serves as a force for good. It's about embracing the responsibility that comes with this knowledge, recognizing that AI's future depends on our collective efforts.

For those who choose to embark on this journey, the rewards are boundless. You will gain a deeper understanding of the world around you, develop valuable skills, and contribute to a future where technology serves as a force for good. It's an invitation to join the conversation, to contribute to the dialogue, and to shape the future of AI for the benefit of all. The N.E.R.D.Y. Way is a testament to the power of learning, collaboration, and continuous exploration, a journey that will enrich your life and help build a better future for everyone.

The N.E.R.D.Y. Way isn't just about understanding AI; it's about becoming a part of its evolution, a contributor to its progress, and a champion for its responsible development and deployment. It's a reminder that the future of AI is not a distant prospect; it's happening now, and it's up to us to shape it. It's a call to action, a reminder that we all have a role to play in this journey, and every step we take, every question we ask, every idea we share, helps us move closer to a brighter future.

CHAPTER 1

THE DAWN OF NEW INTELLIGENCE

WHAT IS AI?

Imagine a world where machines can think, learn, and solve problems just like humans. This is the realm of Artificial Intelligence (AI), a field that's rapidly transforming our lives and shaping the future. AI is not just a futuristic concept; it's already deeply embedded in our everyday experiences, from the personalized recommendations on our favorite streaming services to the voice assistants that answer our questions. But what exactly is AI?

At its core, AI is the simulation of human intelligence processes by computer systems. These systems are designed to perform tasks that typically require human intelligence, such as learning, problem-solving, decision-making, and understanding natural language. AI encompasses a wide spectrum of capabilities, ranging from simple tasks like recognizing patterns in images to complex activities like writing creative content or composing music.

To understand the nuances of AI, it's helpful to visualize it as a spectrum of intelligence, starting with narrow or weak AI and progressing to general and eventually superintelligence.

- **Narrow AI (or Weak AI):** This is the most common type of AI we encounter today. Narrow AI systems are designed to perform specific tasks and excel at those tasks but lack the general intelligence to perform tasks outside their predefined domain. Think of a chess-playing AI, a spam filter, or a self-driving car. These AI systems are highly specialized and operate within a limited scope.
- **General AI (or Strong AI):** This refers to AI systems that possess the same level of cognitive abilities as a human being. General AI systems would be capable of understanding, learning, and performing any intellectual task that a human can, including reasoning, planning, and creative thinking. While general AI remains a distant goal, researchers are constantly pushing the boundaries of AI capabilities.
- **Superintelligence:** This is a hypothetical type of AI that surpasses human intelligence in all aspects. Superintelligence would possess cognitive abilities far exceeding those of any human, capable of understanding and solving problems that are beyond our current grasp. The potential implications of superintelligence are vast and complex, raising philosophical, ethical, and societal questions that require careful consideration.

AI is not a monolithic entity but rather a diverse field encompassing various approaches and techniques. One key aspect of

AI is machine learning, which enables computers to learn from data without explicit programming. Imagine teaching a computer to distinguish between cats and dogs by showing it thousands of images of both animals. Machine learning algorithms can analyze these images, identify patterns, and learn to classify new images as cats or dogs.

Within machine learning, different approaches are used, including supervised learning, unsupervised learning, and reinforcement learning.

- **Supervised Learning:** In supervised learning, AI algorithms are trained on labeled datasets, where each example has a known output. Think of teaching a computer to recognize handwritten digits by showing it images labeled with the corresponding digits. The algorithm learns from these labeled examples and is then able to classify new handwritten digits.
- **Unsupervised Learning:** Unsupervised learning deals with unlabeled data, where the algorithm must discover hidden patterns and structures without explicit guidance. Imagine a system analyzing customer purchase data to identify different customer segments or groups with similar buying habits. The algorithm can cluster customers based on their purchase history, revealing insights that might not be apparent through manual analysis.
- **Reinforcement Learning:** Reinforcement learning is inspired by the concept of trial and error. AI agents interact with their environment, receiving rewards or punishments based on their actions. Through repeated interactions, the agent learns to optimize its behavior

to maximize rewards. Think of a robotic arm learning to pick up objects by trying different movements until it successfully grasps the object.

AI is a rapidly evolving field with a rich history. Its roots can be traced back to the mid-20th century, with early pioneers like Alan Turing, who proposed the Turing Test as a measure of machine intelligence. The Turing Test involves a human evaluator interacting with a machine and a human subject. If the evaluator cannot distinguish between the machine and the human based on their responses, it's considered evidence of machine intelligence.

The field of AI has witnessed significant milestones and paradigm shifts throughout its history, including:

- **The Development of the First AI Programs (1950s-1960s):** This era saw the creation of early AI programs, such as the Logic Theorist and the General Problem Solver, which aimed to demonstrate the capabilities of AI systems in solving logical problems and performing symbolic reasoning.
- **The Rise of Expert Systems (1970s-1980s):** Expert systems emerged as a key application of AI, utilizing knowledge-based approaches to solve problems in specific domains, such as medical diagnosis, financial analysis, and legal advice. These systems were designed to mimic the decision-making processes of human experts.
- **The Era of Machine Learning and Neural Networks (1980s-present):** The development of machine learning algorithms, particularly neural

networks, marked a major turning point in AI. Neural networks are inspired by the structure and function of the human brain, enabling AI systems to learn from data in a more flexible and adaptable manner.

- **The Deep Learning Revolution (2010s-present):** Deep learning, a subfield of machine learning, has driven significant advancements in AI, leading to breakthroughs in areas such as computer vision, natural language processing, and speech recognition. Deep learning algorithms are capable of analyzing complex patterns in data, enabling them to achieve high levels of accuracy in various tasks.

Today, AI is revolutionizing various industries and aspects of our lives. From self-driving cars to personalized medicine, AI is transforming the way we work, live, and interact with the world. AI is also playing a pivotal role in solving global challenges, such as climate change, poverty, and disease.

As AI continues to advance, it raises important ethical considerations. Issues like bias in AI, privacy concerns, and the potential for job displacement require careful attention. It's crucial to ensure that AI is developed and deployed responsibly, promoting fairness, transparency, and human well-being.

Understanding the principles of AI, its capabilities, and its potential impact is essential for everyone, not just experts in the field. AI is shaping the future, and by understanding its foundations, we can all contribute to building a future where AI empowers humanity for the benefit of all.

The History of AI

The story of Artificial Intelligence (AI) is a captivating saga that unfolds like a thrilling novel. It's a tale of bold dreams, ground-breaking breakthroughs, and persistent challenges—a journey that began with the ambition of creating machines capable of mimicking human thought.

The first chapter of this story begins in the mid-20th century, when a visionary mathematician named Alan Turing posed a profound question that would shape the trajectory of AI research: "Can machines think?" This question, crystallized in what we now know as the Turing Test, aimed to establish a standard for assessing a machine's ability to exhibit intelligent behavior indistinguishable from that of a human.

While the Turing Test provided a theoretical framework, it was the pioneering work of John McCarthy, Marvin Minsky, Claude Shannon, and Nathaniel Rochester that truly ignited the flame of AI research. These individuals, convening at Dartmouth College in 1956 for a historic workshop, formally coined the term "Artificial Intelligence." The Dartmouth workshop laid the foundation for a new era of research, fueled by optimism and the belief that machines could be imbued with human-like intelligence.

The early years of AI were characterized by a surge of excitement and remarkable progress. Programs like the Logic Theorist, developed by Allen Newell and Herbert Simon, demonstrated the potential of AI to solve complex problems, even exceeding human capabilities in certain domains. However, this initial euphoria soon gave way to a period of disillusionment known as the "AI winter" (1974-1980).

The early AI programs, often based on symbolic reasoning and limited by the computational power of the time, failed to deliver on their ambitious promises. The limitations of these early systems, coupled with a lack of funding and realistic expectations, led to a significant decline in research interest.

Despite the setbacks, the flame of AI research never truly extinguished. In the 1980s, a resurgence of interest emerged driven by advancements in expert systems, which focused on emulating the knowledge and reasoning capabilities of human experts in specific domains. Expert systems, such as the MYCIN system for diagnosing bacterial infections, found practical applications in medicine, finance, and other fields.

The 1990s witnessed the dawn of a new era in AI—the age of machine learning. Machine learning, a subfield of AI that focuses on enabling computers to learn from data without explicit programming, revolutionized the field. Algorithms like decision trees, support vector machines, and naive Bayes classifiers emerged as powerful tools for analyzing data and making predictions.

The development of the internet and the explosive growth of data availability further fueled the rise of machine learning. From search engines to online recommendations, machine learning algorithms began to permeate our digital lives.

The 2000s ushered in the era of deep learning, a transformative paradigm shift within machine learning. Inspired by the structure of the human brain, deep learning employs artificial neural networks with multiple layers, enabling the analysis of complex patterns in data. Deep learning models have achieved unprecedented breakthroughs in areas like image recognition, natural language processing, and machine translation.

The success of deep learning can be attributed to several factors. First, the availability of massive datasets has provided rich training data for these models. Second, advances in computer hardware, particularly the development of Graphics Processing Units (GPUs), have made it possible to train complex deep learning models efficiently. Third, the emergence of new algorithms and architectures, such as convolutional neural networks and recurrent neural networks, has significantly enhanced the capabilities of deep learning models.

The history of AI is a testament to the enduring power of human ingenuity. From its humble beginnings in the mid-20th century to the transformative impact of deep learning today, AI has consistently pushed the boundaries of what machines can achieve. Yet, this journey has been punctuated by periods of both optimism and skepticism, marked by breakthroughs and challenges.

As we stand at the cusp of an AI-powered future, it's crucial to understand this rich history. By acknowledging the successes, failures, and lessons learned, we can navigate the ethical and societal implications of this transformative technology, shaping a future where AI empowers humanity and enhances our lives.

Types of AI

The realm of Artificial Intelligence (AI) is often shrouded in mystery, a land of advanced algorithms and complex computations. While it might seem daunting, AI is not some futuristic technology reserved for science fiction. It's woven into the fabric of our daily lives, influencing everything from the recommendations we see on streaming platforms to the navigation routes on our smartphones. To grasp the full potential of AI, we need to first understand its different forms, each with its unique strengths and limitations.

Imagine a spectrum of intelligence, where at one end lies the simple intelligence of a calculator, capable only of basic calculations. As we move along this spectrum, we encounter more complex forms of intelligence, culminating in the advanced capabilities of the human mind. This spectrum provides a framework for categorizing the different types of AI, from the limited intelligence of narrow AI to the hypothetical possibilities of general and superintelligence.

1.3.1 Narrow AI: The Specialized Problem Solvers

Narrow AI, also known as Weak AI, is the most prevalent type of AI we encounter today. It excels at performing specific tasks, often within a predefined range of parameters. Think of a chess-playing program; it can defeat even the most skilled human players but is limited to the game of chess. Narrow AI applications are abundant in our daily lives, quietly working behind the scenes to make our experiences more convenient and efficient.

Take, for instance, the ubiquitous voice assistants like Siri, Alexa, and Google Assistant. These AI systems are designed to understand and respond to natural language commands, providing information, controlling smart home devices, and playing music. They are highly specialized in their tasks, excelling in speech recognition and language processing but lacking the ability to generalize their knowledge to other domains.

Another example is the spam filter in your email inbox. This narrow AI system analyzes patterns in emails, identifying and blocking messages likely to be spam. Its focus is narrow, limited to the task of identifying unwanted emails and requiring constant training to adapt to evolving spam techniques.

1.3.2 General AI: The Human-Like Intelligence

While narrow AI excels at specific tasks, general AI, or strong AI, aspires to possess the same breadth of intelligence as a human being. It aims to understand and reason about the world, learn new concepts, and adapt to changing circumstances with the same flexibility as a human.

Imagine an AI system capable of performing any intellectual task that a human can, from writing a novel to composing a symphony. This hypothetical general AI would not be limited to specific tasks but would possess the cognitive abilities to learn, adapt, and solve problems across diverse domains.

The development of general AI remains a significant challenge, requiring advancements in fields like cognitive science, psychology, and neuroscience. Despite its elusive nature, general AI holds the promise of transforming our world, creating new possibilities in various fields, from scientific research to creative endeavors.

1.3.3 Superintelligence: The Intelligence Beyond Human Limits

If general AI represents the ambition to replicate human intelligence, superintelligence takes this concept to a new level, envisioning AI surpassing human cognitive abilities in every aspect. This hypothetical form of AI would not only possess human-like intelligence but would also exceed it, capable of solving complex problems, understanding abstract concepts, and making decisions with unparalleled efficiency.

The potential benefits of superintelligence are vast, ranging from curing diseases and solving environmental challenges to advancing scientific discovery at an unprecedented pace. However, the development of superintelligence also raises concerns about its potential risks and the need for careful ethical considerations.

1.3.4 The Landscape of AI: A Spectrum of Possibilities

As we navigate the landscape of AI, it's essential to remember that these categories represent a spectrum of possibilities, not rigid boundaries. Narrow AI might be capable of learning and adapting within its specific domain, exhibiting a degree of general intelligence within its limited scope. Similarly, general AI might emerge gradually, starting with AI systems that possess some human-like cognitive abilities before achieving true general intelligence.

The progression from narrow AI to general AI and beyond is a journey of technological advancement, driven by continuous innovation and a growing understanding of intelligence. While the path to general and superintelligence may be long and uncertain, the journey itself is profoundly transformative, shaping the way we live, work, and interact with the world around us.

1.3.5 The Ethical Considerations of AI: A Balancing Act

The development of advanced AI raises ethical considerations that must be addressed with utmost care. As AI systems become more sophisticated, it is crucial to ensure their alignment with human values, preventing unintended consequences and promoting the well-being of all.

One key ethical concern is the potential for bias in AI algorithms. AI systems learn from data, and if the data contains biases, these biases will be reflected in the AI's decision-making. It is vital to develop AI systems that are fair, unbiased, and equitable, ensuring that all individuals are treated fairly regardless of their background or characteristics.

Another crucial ethical consideration is data privacy and security. AI systems rely heavily on data, and it is essential to protect individuals' privacy and ensure that sensitive information is not misused. Implementing strong data privacy policies and ensuring responsible data management are crucial for building trust in AI systems.

As AI continues to evolve, it is crucial to engage in ongoing discussions about its ethical implications. By fostering responsible AI development and deployment, we can harness its potential for good while mitigating its potential risks, shaping a future where AI empowers humanity and benefits all.

This is not just about the technology; it's about the impact AI has on our lives. As AI continues to evolve, we must be vigilant in ensuring that it aligns with our values and serves the greater good. The future of AI is not predetermined; it's a journey we must navigate together, embracing its potential while remaining conscious of its challenges.

1.4 AI in Action

Imagine a world where your smartphone anticipates your needs before you even ask. A world where personalized recommendations for movies, music, and products appear seamlessly on your screen. This isn't science fiction; it's the reality of Artificial Intelligence (AI) woven into the fabric of our daily lives.

AI, in its various forms, silently assists us in countless ways, from the mundane to the extraordinary. It's the unseen hand that guides us through the digital world, making it easier to navigate, learn, and connect. Let's embark on a journey to explore how AI is shaping our experiences, one interaction at a time.

The Invisible AI Assistant: Personalized Recommendations

Picture yourself browsing your favorite online shopping platform. As you scroll through products, a curated selection appears, tailored to your preferences. This isn't magic; it's AI-powered recommendation systems at work.

These intelligent algorithms analyze your past browsing history, purchase patterns, and even your online behavior. They learn from your interactions and use that knowledge to predict what you'll be interested in next. This personalized touch makes shopping more efficient and enjoyable, ensuring you discover products that align with your tastes.

But AI's influence goes beyond just suggesting items. It's behind the personalized playlists curated by music streaming services like Spotify and Apple Music. These platforms analyze your listening habits, noting your favorite artists, genres, and even the time of day you listen. Based on this data, AI creates unique playlists that cater to your musical tastes and mood.

Similarly, AI-powered movie and TV show recommendations on streaming services like Netflix and Amazon Prime Video are based on your viewing history, ratings, and even the genres you tend to gravitate towards. These systems are constantly learning, refining their recommendations to provide you with the most enjoyable viewing experience.

Voice Assistants: Your Digital Companions

From asking questions to setting reminders, voice assistants like Siri, Alexa, and Google Assistant have become ubiquitous in our lives. These AI-powered companions listen to our commands, understand our requests, and execute tasks accordingly.

The magic behind voice assistants lies in natural language processing (NLP), a field of AI that enables computers to understand and interact with human language. These assistants can analyze the nuances of our speech, recognizing accents, slang, and even sarcasm. They then use this information to interpret our requests and provide accurate responses.

But the capabilities of voice assistants extend far beyond simple tasks. They can act as personal assistants, scheduling appointments, sending messages, and even controlling smart home devices. Some can even engage in basic conversations, providing companionship and entertainment.

Search Engines: Unlocking Information at Your Fingertips

Search engines like Google, Bing, and DuckDuckGo are the gateways to the vast digital world. With each query we enter, AI works behind the scenes to deliver relevant results. These intelligent algorithms analyze the billions of web pages available, identifying those that best match our search terms.

AI's role in search engines extends beyond simple keyword matching. They understand the context of our searches, recognizing synonyms, identifying related topics, and even predicting what we might be looking for before we even type it. This advanced understanding allows search engines to provide more accurate and comprehensive results, making it easier for us to find the information we need.

Social Media: Connecting and Engaging

Social media platforms like Facebook, Instagram, and Twitter utilize AI to personalize our feeds, suggest friends, and even identify potential threats. These algorithms analyze our interactions, likes, and comments to create a curated experience tailored to our interests.

AI also plays a crucial role in combating misinformation and harmful content. By analyzing posts and comments, AI can detect and flag potentially offensive or misleading information, promoting a safer and more positive environment for users.

AI in the World Around Us

AI's impact stretches beyond our digital lives, permeating various aspects of our physical world.

- **Transportation:** Self-driving cars, powered by AI, are becoming increasingly common. These vehicles use sensors, cameras, and sophisticated algorithms to navigate roads, avoid obstacles, and make real-time driving decisions.
- **Healthcare:** AI is revolutionizing healthcare, aiding in disease diagnosis, drug discovery, and personalized treatment plans. It's even being used to develop new medical technologies, like robotic surgery systems and AI-powered prosthetics.
- **Security:** AI-powered surveillance systems are being deployed to enhance security in public spaces, detecting suspicious activity and providing real-time alerts. AI is also being used to develop sophisticated cybersecurity systems to combat cyber threats.

AI: A Force for Good

While AI has the potential to be a transformative force in our lives, it's crucial to address the ethical considerations surrounding its development and deployment. We must strive to ensure AI is used responsibly, ethically, and in a way that benefits society as a whole.

By understanding the fundamentals of AI, its applications, and its potential impact, we can shape its trajectory, ensuring it serves as a force for good in our world.

This journey into AI is just beginning. As we delve deeper, we'll uncover the complexities, challenges, and possibilities that lie ahead. Let's explore this fascinating world together, embracing the opportunities and navigating the challenges with open minds and a shared desire to harness the power of AI for a brighter future.

THE FUTURE OF AI

The future of AI is a tapestry woven with threads of wonder and apprehension, a landscape brimming with potential for both progress and peril. It's a future where AI, having shed its nascent shell, will blossom into a force capable of reshaping the very fabric of human existence.

Imagine a world where self-driving cars seamlessly navigate our streets, guided by intelligent algorithms that prioritize safety and efficiency. Where healthcare is personalized, with AI-powered diagnostics uncovering hidden ailments and treatment plans tailored to individual needs. A world where education is customized, with AI tutors adapting to each student's unique learning style, fostering a love of knowledge and unlocking hidden potential. These are just glimpses into the transformative potential of AI, a power that could revolutionize industries, enhance productivity, and improve the quality of life for millions.

Yet, with this burgeoning power comes an imperative for responsible stewardship. The ethical considerations surrounding AI's development and deployment cannot be ignored. As AI increasingly infiltrates our lives, we must grapple with questions of bias, privacy, and the very nature of our relationship with machines. The future of AI is not predetermined. It is a future we must shape together, ensuring that this powerful technology serves as a force for good, empowering humanity and fostering a brighter future for all.

The Rise of Intelligent Machines

The transformative potential of AI extends far beyond the realm of our everyday lives. Industries ranging from finance and healthcare to manufacturing and transportation are poised to be revolutionized by AI-driven innovations.

In finance, AI algorithms are already transforming investment strategies, detecting fraud, and enhancing cybersecurity. They can analyze vast amounts of data to identify market trends, predict price fluctuations, and optimize portfolio allocation, empowering investors to make more informed decisions. AI-powered chatbots are also revolutionizing customer service, providing instant support and resolving queries with unparalleled efficiency.

Healthcare, too, is being reshaped by AI. Algorithms can now assist in diagnosing diseases with greater accuracy than human doctors, analyzing medical images to detect tumors and other anomalies. AI is also playing a crucial role in drug discovery, identifying promising new drug candidates and accelerating the development of life-saving treatments. AI-powered robots are even being used to assist surgeons in complex procedures, enhancing precision and improving patient outcomes.

The manufacturing industry is undergoing a similar AI-driven transformation. Robots powered by AI are automating repetitive tasks on factory floors, boosting productivity and improving efficiency. AI algorithms are also being used to optimize production processes, reducing waste and minimizing downtime. This shift towards automation is not only making manufacturing more efficient but also creating new opportunities for workers to focus on higher-value tasks.

The world of transportation is also on the cusp of a revolutionary shift. Self-driving cars, powered by AI algorithms that perceive their surroundings and make decisions in real-time, are poised to transform the way we travel. These vehicles have the potential to significantly improve road safety, reduce traffic congestion, and create new mobility options for those who are unable to drive. AI is also playing a crucial role in air traffic management, optimizing flight paths and reducing delays.

Ethical Considerations: Navigating the Crossroads

As AI becomes increasingly sophisticated and pervasive, its ethical implications become increasingly complex. This raises a crucial question: how can we ensure that AI is used for good, promoting societal progress while safeguarding human values?

One of the most pressing concerns is the potential for bias in AI algorithms. AI systems are trained on vast datasets, and if these datasets contain biases, the AI will inevitably reflect them. For instance, a facial recognition system trained on a dataset predominantly featuring white faces might be less accurate when identifying individuals with darker skin tones. This type of bias can have real-world consequences, leading to discrimination and unfair treatment.

To mitigate this risk, we need to develop AI systems that are fair and unbiased. This involves carefully curating datasets, ensuring they are diverse and representative of the population they are intended to serve. It also requires developing algorithms that are more robust to bias and can detect and correct for unfair outcomes.

Privacy and security are also paramount concerns in the era of AI. AI systems often require access to vast amounts of personal data, raising questions about data ownership and consent. How can we protect individuals' privacy while allowing AI to harness the power of data for good?

One approach is to develop privacy-preserving techniques, such as differential privacy, which allows data to be analyzed without revealing sensitive information about individuals. It also requires robust security measures to protect data from unauthorized access and cyberattacks.

The rise of AI also raises questions about the future of work. Some experts predict that AI will lead to widespread job displacement, as machines take over tasks currently performed by humans. However, others argue that AI will create new jobs and enhance existing ones, leading to a more dynamic and collaborative work environment.

To navigate this complex landscape, we need to prepare for the changing job market by fostering a culture of lifelong learning and reskilling. We must invest in education and training programs that equip individuals with the skills necessary to thrive in an AI-powered world.

The Human-AI Partnership: A Journey of Collaboration

The future of AI is not solely about machines replacing humans. It is about a new era of collaboration, where humans and AI work together to achieve greater heights. This partnership can unlock unprecedented possibilities, allowing us to solve complex problems and create a better future for all.

AI can augment our capabilities, enhancing our decision-making, problem-solving, and creative abilities. By taking on repetitive and mundane tasks, AI can free up human ingenuity for higher-level activities that require creativity, empathy, and critical thinking.

Imagine a world where AI assists scientists in developing life-saving drugs, where AI empowers artists to create innovative works of art, and where AI helps educators personalize learning for every student. These are just a few examples of how AI can empower humanity, unlocking our full potential and driving progress across every facet of human endeavor.

Shaping the Future: A Call to Action

The future of AI is a blank canvas, and we, as individuals, have a crucial role to play in shaping its trajectory. It's our responsibility to engage with this powerful technology, explore its possibilities, and ensure it serves as a force for good.

We can embrace AI as a tool for progress, harnessing its power to address global challenges like climate change, poverty, and disease. We can invest in research and development to ensure that AI is ethical, fair, and safe. And we can advocate for policies that promote responsible AI development and deployment.

The journey into the AI era is not without its uncertainties. But with a commitment to ethical development, responsible use, and a spirit of collaboration, we can navigate the challenges and harness the immense potential of AI to build a brighter future for all. This is the N.E.R.D.Y. way, a journey of discovery, innovation, and empowerment, where technology empowers humanity to create a world where we can all thrive.

CHAPTER 2

UNLOCKING THE POWER OF DATA

DATA

Imagine a world where computers can learn, adapt, and make decisions—not through explicit programming, but by analyzing vast amounts of data. This is the realm of Artificial Intelligence (AI), and at its heart lies the power of data. Like a sculptor molding clay, data shapes and guides AI algorithms, enabling them to perform extraordinary feats.

Think of AI algorithms as sophisticated tools that need to be trained to understand patterns, make predictions, and solve problems. This training process is like educating a child—it requires a constant stream of information, examples, and experiences. The more data we feed these algorithms, the better they become at their tasks, just as a child learns more with exposure to a diverse range of knowledge.

Data fuels the learning process, guiding AI algorithms to recognize intricate relationships and make informed decisions. Consider a medical AI system designed to diagnose diseases based on patient data. This system needs to be trained on vast amounts of medical records, including patient demographics, symptoms, test results, and diagnoses. By analyzing these patterns, the AI can learn to identify disease markers, predict potential complications, and suggest appropriate treatments.

But the power of data goes far beyond simple pattern recognition. AI algorithms can be trained to handle complex tasks such as natural language processing, image recognition, and autonomous navigation. These applications require vast amounts of data to learn the intricacies of human language, the complexities of visual perception, and the nuances of navigating real-world environments.

Take, for example, a self-driving car. To navigate safely, it needs to learn from a massive dataset of real-world driving scenarios, including road conditions, traffic patterns, pedestrian behavior, and weather changes. This training data allows the car's AI to anticipate obstacles, optimize driving routes, and make real-time decisions, mimicking the cognitive abilities of a human driver.

The importance of data in AI is undeniable. It's the lifeblood that fuels the learning process, enabling algorithms to adapt, evolve, and become more sophisticated. But it's important to recognize the different types of data that power AI systems.

Data can be broadly categorized as structured and unstructured. Structured data is neatly organized and formatted, typically found in databases and spreadsheets. Examples include customer information, financial transactions, and sensor readings. Unstructured data, on the other hand, is raw and unorganized, such as text documents, images, audio recordings, and video files.

AI algorithms can process both structured and unstructured data to gain insights. For instance, a chatbot trained on structured customer service data can efficiently answer common questions and resolve simple issues. However, to understand the nuances of human language and engage in more complex conversations, the chatbot also needs to be trained on unstructured data, such as text transcripts of real conversations.

To effectively leverage the power of data in AI, it's crucial to acquire and prepare this data properly. This process, known as data acquisition and preprocessing, involves collecting raw data from various sources, cleaning it to remove errors and inconsistencies, and transforming it into a format suitable for AI algorithms.

Imagine collecting customer feedback data from different channels, including online reviews, social media posts, and customer support logs. This data needs to be cleaned and standardized, removing irrelevant information and inconsistencies in format. The preprocessing step ensures that the AI algorithm can efficiently analyze the data and extract meaningful insights.

Once data is acquired and preprocessed, AI algorithms can analyze and visualize it to identify patterns and trends that might not be readily apparent. Data visualization techniques, such as charts, graphs, and maps, enable us to understand complex data relationships and make informed decisions.

Consider an AI system used to analyze customer purchasing patterns. By visualizing this data, we can identify popular products, understand customer preferences, and predict future trends. These insights can inform marketing strategies, product development, and inventory management, ultimately improving customer satisfaction and driving business success.

While data plays a vital role in AI, its power also comes with ethical considerations. We must navigate the challenges of data privacy, bias, and responsible use to ensure that AI is deployed for good.

Data privacy is paramount in the age of AI. As AI systems collect and analyze vast amounts of personal information, we need to ensure that this data is handled responsibly and ethically. This involves implementing robust security measures, obtaining informed consent, and limiting the collection and use of sensitive data.

Bias in AI is another crucial ethical concern. AI algorithms can perpetuate existing societal biases if they are trained on datasets that reflect those biases. This can lead to unfair outcomes and exacerbate inequalities.

Imagine an AI system used to predict loan eligibility, trained on historical data that shows racial biases in lending practices. This system could inadvertently perpetuate those biases, denying loans to individuals based on their race rather than their credit-worthiness.

To mitigate bias in AI, it's essential to use diverse and representative datasets, develop algorithms that are robust to bias, and implement mechanisms for detecting and correcting bias.

Finally, responsible data use is crucial for ensuring that AI is deployed for the benefit of humanity. We need to consider the potential consequences of using AI in various applications, from healthcare to law enforcement, and strive to mitigate any negative impacts.

For instance, AI systems used in criminal justice need to be carefully designed and tested to ensure fairness and accuracy. We need to address concerns about potential bias in facial recognition systems, the impact of AI-powered surveillance systems on privacy, and the potential for AI to be used for malicious purposes.

Data is the lifeblood of AI, powering its learning and driving its performance. By understanding the different types of data, mastering data acquisition and preprocessing, and embracing data visualization techniques, we can unlock the transformative potential of AI. But we must also navigate the ethical landscape of data use with care, ensuring that AI is deployed responsibly and for the good of all.

Types of Data

Data is the lifeblood of AI. Just as our bodies need food, water, and oxygen to function, AI systems rely on data to learn, grow, and perform their tasks. Without data, AI algorithms are like empty vessels, lacking the information they need to develop intelligence and solve problems.

Imagine a chef trying to create a delicious meal without any ingredients. The chef might have a recipe, but without the necessary ingredients, they can't create anything. Similarly, an AI system without data is limited in its ability to learn and solve problems.

This is where the concept of "data as the fuel of AI" comes into play. Just as fuel powers a car, data fuels the engine of AI. Every piece of data, whether it's a customer's purchase history, a medical record, or a satellite image, provides AI systems with valuable insights and allows them to learn and adapt.

But data isn't just a generic fuel; it comes in many forms, each with its unique properties and uses. Understanding these different types of data is crucial for anyone working with AI, as it allows us to harness the power of data more effectively and unlock its full potential.

Structured Data: Order and Organization

Structured data is like a well-organized pantry, where every item has its place and is easily accessible. It follows a predefined format, typically stored in tables with rows and columns, making it easy to analyze and process. Think of a spreadsheet with neatly arranged data points, each representing a specific attribute or characteristic.

Here are some examples of structured data:

- **Customer databases:** Tables containing information about customers, such as their names, addresses, purchase history, and contact details.
- **Financial records:** Tables containing information about financial transactions, such as stock prices, bank balances, and investment portfolios.
- **Inventory management systems:** Tables containing information about products, such as their names, descriptions, quantities, and prices.

Structured data is ideal for tasks that require precise analysis and calculations, such as:

- **Predictive analytics:** Forecasting future trends and outcomes based on historical data, like predicting customer churn or stock market movements.

- **Business intelligence:** Analyzing business data to identify patterns and insights that can improve operations and decision-making.
- **Machine learning models:** Training AI models to make predictions or classifications based on structured data, like identifying fraudulent transactions or predicting customer preferences.

Unstructured Data: The Wild West of Information

Unstructured data, on the other hand, is like a vast and untamed landscape, full of diverse and unorganized information. It doesn't conform to a predefined format and is typically found in formats such as text documents, images, videos, and audio recordings.

Here are some examples of unstructured data:

- **Social media posts:** Text, images, and videos shared on platforms like Facebook, Twitter, and Instagram.
- **Email messages:** Text-based communication between individuals and organizations.
- **Customer reviews:** Text-based feedback from customers about products or services.
- **Medical images:** X-rays, CT scans, and MRIs used for diagnosis and treatment.
- **Audio recordings:** Speech recordings, music, and podcasts.

Unstructured data presents unique challenges for AI systems, as it requires sophisticated techniques to extract meaningful insights. This is where natural language processing (NLP), computer vision, and other specialized AI techniques come into play.

Here are some examples of how AI is used to analyze unstructured data:

- **Sentiment analysis:** Analyzing text data to understand the emotions and opinions expressed, such as determining customer satisfaction or identifying potential risks.
- **Image recognition:** Identifying objects and patterns in images, such as detecting tumors in medical images or recognizing faces in security footage.
- **Speech recognition:** Converting audio recordings into text, enabling AI systems to understand spoken language and transcribe conversations.

Semi-structured Data: Finding the Middle Ground

Semi-structured data sits in the middle ground between structured and unstructured data. It has some degree of organization, but it doesn't follow a rigid format like structured data. Think of it as a partially organized pantry, where some items are neatly arranged while others are scattered.

Here are some examples of semi-structured data:

- **XML files:** Data stored in a hierarchical structure, often used for configuration files and web services.
- **JSON files:** Data stored in a key-value pair format, commonly used for web applications and data exchange.

- **Log files:** Records of events and activities within a system, containing information about user actions, system performance, and errors.

Semi-structured data offers a balance between the structured approach of relational databases and the flexibility of unstructured data. It can be processed using both structured and unstructured data analysis techniques.

The Importance of Understanding Different Data Types

Understanding the different types of data is crucial for working with AI, as it helps us to:

- **Choose the right AI tools and techniques:** Different data types require different tools and techniques for analysis. For example, structured data can be analyzed using relational databases and SQL queries, while unstructured data requires techniques like NLP or computer vision.
- **Extract valuable insights from data:** By understanding the characteristics of different data types, we can develop strategies for extracting meaningful insights.
- **Ensure the quality and accuracy of data:** Different data types have different sources and characteristics, and it's important to ensure that data is accurate, complete, and relevant for AI analysis.
- **Address ethical considerations:** Different data types have different implications for privacy, bias, and security, and it's important to address these considerations before using data for AI applications.

Data Types in Action: Real-World Examples

To illustrate the different types of data and their uses in AI, let's consider a few real-world examples.

Example 1: Predicting Customer Churn

A telecommunications company wants to predict which customers are likely to cancel their service. They have a database containing structured data about their customers, such as their age, location, service plan, and billing history. They can use this data to train a machine learning model to predict customer churn.

Example 2: Diagnosing Diseases from Medical Images

A hospital wants to use AI to diagnose lung cancer from CT scans. They have a large collection of medical images, both normal and cancerous, which they can use to train a computer vision model to identify patterns associated with cancer.

Example 3: Personalizing Learning Experiences

An educational platform wants to personalize learning experiences for students based on their individual needs and learning styles. They can use data from student interactions, assessments, and feedback to create AI-powered learning paths that adapt to each student's progress and preferences.

The Evolution of Data: From Structured to Unstructured

As AI continues to evolve, the types of data used for AI applications are also changing. Initially, AI systems primarily relied on structured data, but as AI techniques have advanced, the use of unstructured data has become increasingly prevalent.

This shift is due to the growing availability of unstructured data from sources like social media, sensor networks, and the internet of things. AI systems are now able to process and analyze massive amounts of unstructured data, unlocking insights and capabilities that were previously impossible.

The future of AI will likely see a further blurring of the lines between structured and unstructured data, as new data sources emerge and AI techniques become more sophisticated. It's an exciting time for anyone working with data and AI, as we continue to explore the possibilities of this transformative technology.

DATA ACQUISITION AND PREPROCESSING

Imagine you're a detective on a mission to solve a complex case. You arrive at the crime scene, but all you see is a jumble of clues, scattered and seemingly meaningless. To make sense of the situation, you need to gather all the pieces, organize them, and analyze them carefully. This is precisely what happens with raw data in the world of AI.

Data is the lifeblood of AI, fueling its algorithms and enabling them to learn, make predictions, and solve problems. But raw data, like the scattered clues at a crime scene, is often chaotic, incomplete, and messy. It needs to be meticulously collected, cleaned, and transformed into meaningful information before it can be used effectively by AI systems. This crucial process, known as **data acquisition and preprocessing**, is like sifting through the clutter of a crime scene to reveal the vital clues.

The Journey Begins: Data Acquisition

The first step in unlocking the power of data is acquiring it. This involves gathering data from various sources, like online databases, sensors, social media platforms, or even human interactions. The challenge lies in identifying the right sources and ensuring the data collected is relevant, accurate, and complete. Imagine a detective searching for evidence at multiple locations, carefully documenting everything they find.

Think about the various ways data is collected:

- **Websites and applications:** Every time you visit a website or use an app, you leave a digital footprint. Websites and applications track your browsing behavior, purchase history, and interactions, generating valuable data for businesses and AI systems.
- **Sensors:** From smartphones and smartwatches to industrial machines and environmental monitoring stations, sensors are everywhere, collecting data on motion, temperature, light, and more. This data is crucial for AI systems to understand and respond to the physical world.
- **Social media platforms:** Social media platforms like Facebook, Twitter, and Instagram are treasure troves of data. They collect information on your likes, comments, posts, and connections, providing insights into user behavior and social trends.
- **Surveys and questionnaires:** Surveys and questionnaires are a valuable way to gather data directly from people. They can be used to understand public opinion, gather feedback on products or services, or collect information about health and well-being.

Cleaning Up the Mess: Data Preprocessing

Once the raw data is acquired, it needs to be cleaned and preprocessed to ensure its quality and suitability for AI analysis. Imagine the detective meticulously examining the evidence, cleaning it up, and preparing it for analysis. This process, called **data preprocessing**, involves several crucial steps:

- **Data Cleaning:** This step involves removing errors, inconsistencies, and outliers from the dataset. Imagine a detective discarding a broken or misleading clue to ensure they are working with reliable information.
- **Data Transformation:** This step involves converting raw data into a format that is easier to analyze. Imagine the detective organizing the collected evidence into categories, creating a more organized and understandable picture.
- **Data Reduction:** This step involves reducing the size of the dataset without losing valuable information. Think of the detective focusing on the most relevant evidence, discarding irrelevant information to streamline the analysis.
- **Data Imputation:** Sometimes, datasets may contain missing values. Data imputation involves replacing these missing values with reasonable estimates, filling in the gaps to create a more complete picture. Imagine the detective carefully inferring missing details from the available evidence, piecing together a more complete understanding of the situation.

Here's an example to illustrate the importance of data preprocessing: Imagine you're using AI to analyze customer data for a retail company. You collect data on customer purchases, but the data contains errors, like duplicate entries, missing values, and inconsistent data formats. This messy data will hinder the performance of your AI system. To ensure accurate results, you need to clean and preprocess the data, removing errors, standardizing data formats, and filling in missing values.

Types of Data Preprocessing Techniques

Let's delve into some common data preprocessing techniques:

Data Cleaning

- **Missing Value Imputation:** As mentioned earlier, data imputation involves replacing missing values with reasonable estimates. Different methods can be used based on the nature of the data and the missing value pattern. Some common methods include mean imputation, median imputation, and mode imputation, where missing values are replaced with the mean, median, or mode of the respective column.
- **Outlier Detection and Removal:** Outliers are data points that significantly deviate from the rest of the dataset. They can distort AI models and negatively impact analysis. Techniques like box plots, Z-score calculations, and IQR (interquartile range) can be used to identify outliers. Outliers can be removed, replaced, or handled with more sophisticated techniques depending on the context.
- **Data Standardization:** When datasets contain variables with different scales, data standardization helps bring them to a common scale. This is important for algorithms that are sensitive to the scale of features.

Common techniques include Z-score standardization and Min-Max scaling.

Data Transformation

- **Data Encoding:** When dealing with categorical data (like gender, city, or product category), it needs to be converted into a numerical format for AI algorithms to process. Techniques like one-hot encoding and label encoding are commonly used for this purpose.
- **Data Discretization:** This technique involves grouping continuous data into discrete intervals, simplifying the analysis. Imagine categorizing customer ages into age groups like "Young Adults," "Middle Aged," and "Senior Citizens" for easier analysis.

Data Reduction

- **Feature Selection:** When a dataset contains numerous features, some may be irrelevant or redundant. Feature selection techniques aim to identify and remove these unnecessary features, streamlining analysis and improving model performance. Think of the detective carefully selecting the most relevant clues, discarding those that don't contribute to solving the case.
- **Dimensionality Reduction:** Techniques like Principal Component Analysis (PCA) and Linear Discriminant Analysis (LDA) reduce the dimensionality of data by identifying the most important features. They project data into a lower-dimensional space while retaining most of the original information.

The Importance of Data Preprocessing

Data preprocessing is an essential step in the AI workflow for several reasons:

- **Improved Model Performance:** Clean and preprocessed data leads to more accurate and reliable AI models. By removing errors, inconsistencies, and irrelevant information, the AI system can focus on the most relevant data, resulting in better predictions and analysis.
- **Reduced Bias:** Unprocessed data often contains biases, which can lead to unfair outcomes from AI models. Proper preprocessing techniques like outlier detection and data standardization help mitigate these biases, ensuring fairness and equity.
- **Enhanced Data Understanding:** Data preprocessing can help uncover hidden patterns and relationships within the data, providing valuable insights for decision-making.
- **Faster Model Training:** Clean and preprocessed data is easier and faster to train AI models on. This reduces the time and computational resources needed for model development.

Data preprocessing is an essential stage in the AI pipeline, just like meticulously preparing the evidence before a detective can solve a case. It ensures that the data is ready for analysis, leading to more accurate, reliable, and insightful results.

Data Preprocessing in Action

Let's explore a few real-world examples of data preprocessing in action:

- **Healthcare:** AI systems used for diagnosing diseases or predicting patient outcomes rely heavily on data from patient records, medical imaging, and clinical trials. Before this data can be used, it needs to be cleaned, standardized, and transformed to remove errors, inconsistencies, and irrelevant information. This ensures the AI system can make accurate diagnoses and predictions based on reliable data.
- **E-commerce:** AI systems used for recommending products, personalizing customer experiences, or detecting fraudulent transactions rely on data from customer purchases, browsing behavior, and interactions. Data preprocessing is crucial for ensuring the data is accurate, consistent, and free from bias.
- **Finance:** AI systems used for detecting financial fraud, predicting stock prices, or providing personalized financial advice rely on data from transactions, market trends, and customer profiles. Data preprocessing is essential for ensuring the data is clean, accurate, and relevant to the specific financial task.

The Power of Data Preprocessing

Data preprocessing is an essential step in the AI pipeline, allowing AI systems to effectively learn, analyze, and make predictions based on high-quality data. Just as a detective meticulously prepares evidence, data preprocessing prepares the data for AI to unravel its secrets and unlock its power.

DATA VISUALIZATION

Imagine you're presented with a mountain of data, a vast ocean of information. It's raw, unstructured, and seemingly overwhelming. How do you navigate this sea of data to extract valuable insights, uncover hidden patterns, and make sense of the chaos? This is where data visualization steps in as a powerful tool, transforming data into meaningful visual representations that unlock hidden stories.

Data visualization is the art and science of presenting data in a visual format, using charts, graphs, maps, and other visual elements to convey complex information in an easily digestible way. AI, with its ability to process vast amounts of data, plays a pivotal role in shaping and enhancing data visualization techniques. By using AI-powered tools and algorithms, we can go beyond traditional visualizations and create dynamic, interactive, and insightful representations that reveal the hidden stories within data.

AI-Powered Data Visualization: Unlocking the Secrets of Data

Think of data visualization as a bridge between the world of raw data and the world of human understanding. Humans are inherently visual creatures; our brains are wired to process information more effectively when presented visually. Data visualization takes advantage of this innate human ability, transforming abstract data into readily comprehensible visual narratives.

AI enhances data visualization by automating the process of data cleaning, preparation, and analysis. It allows us to create visualizations that are not only visually appealing but also highly insightful. AI-powered data visualization tools offer advanced features like:

- **Automatic Chart Selection:** AI algorithms can analyze the structure and characteristics of your data and suggest the most appropriate chart types, like bar charts, line graphs, scatter plots, or heatmaps, to effectively represent the data.
- **Interactive Visualization:** AI enables dynamic and interactive visualizations, allowing users to explore data from different angles, zoom in on specific areas, filter data points, and uncover insights that might be missed in static visualizations.
- **Real-time Data Updates:** AI can continuously update visualizations with real-time data, allowing users to track trends, monitor performance, and make data-driven decisions in dynamic environments.

Examples of AI-Powered Data Visualization in Action

Let's consider some real-world examples of how AI is transforming the field of data visualization:

- **Healthcare:** Imagine a hospital using AI to analyze patient data and create interactive visualizations that highlight potential risks, disease patterns, and treatment outcomes. This empowers doctors to make more informed decisions, personalize treatment plans, and improve patient care.
- **Finance:** AI-powered data visualization can be used to track market trends, analyze stock performance, identify fraudulent activity, and create interactive

dashboards that provide financial analysts with a comprehensive view of their portfolio.

- **Marketing:** AI can analyze customer data and create interactive dashboards that show customer demographics, purchase history, and engagement patterns, allowing marketers to personalize campaigns, target specific customer segments, and measure the effectiveness of their strategies.
- **Environmental Science:** AI can analyze data from satellites, weather stations, and other sources to create interactive maps that show environmental trends, pollution levels, and climate change patterns, helping scientists understand and address these critical issues.

Key Data Visualization Techniques Enhanced by AI

AI plays a crucial role in enhancing various data visualization techniques, helping us create more insightful, engaging, and actionable visualizations:

- **Clustering:** AI algorithms like k-means clustering can identify groups of similar data points, allowing you to create visualizations that highlight distinct patterns and relationships within your dataset. For instance, you could cluster customers based on their purchasing behavior, revealing distinct segments with different needs and preferences.
- **Dimensionality Reduction:** AI techniques like Principal Component Analysis (PCA) can reduce the dimensionality of data, enabling you to visualize complex datasets in lower-dimensional spaces. This helps us identify key patterns and

trends without being overwhelmed by a high volume of data.

- **Network Graphs:** AI can analyze relationships and connections within data to create network graphs that reveal intricate patterns and connections. These graphs can be used to visualize social networks, network security, or the spread of information.
- **Time Series Visualization:** AI can analyze time series data to identify trends, seasonality, and anomalies. This allows us to create interactive visualizations that show how data changes over time, enabling us to monitor performance, forecast future trends, and make informed decisions based on historical patterns.
- **Geospatial Visualization:** AI can process location data to create interactive maps that show the distribution of data points across geographical regions. This enables us to analyze spatial patterns, identify areas of interest, and understand the impact of various factors on different locations.

The Future of Data Visualization: A World of Insights

AI is not only enhancing existing data visualization techniques but also opening up new possibilities for data exploration and understanding. Here are some exciting trends in the future of AI-powered data visualization:

- **Explainable AI (XAI):** AI models are becoming more transparent and interpretable, allowing users to understand the reasoning behind the visualizations and gain insights into the decision-making process. This is essential for building trust in AI-powered insights.

- **Augmented Reality (AR) and Virtual Reality (VR):** AI-powered data visualization will become more immersive, using AR and VR to create interactive, three-dimensional representations of data, allowing users to explore and analyze data in a more engaging and intuitive way.
- **Natural Language Processing (NLP):** AI will be able to interpret natural language queries and translate complex data into easy-to-understand visualizations. This will make data visualization accessible to a wider audience, even those without technical expertise.
- **Personalization:** AI will personalize data visualizations based on user preferences, data context, and specific tasks, ensuring that each visualization is relevant and actionable.

In a world flooded with data, data visualization plays a crucial role in helping us navigate the information overload and uncover meaningful insights. AI is revolutionizing this field, providing us with powerful tools and techniques to create more insightful, interactive, and dynamic visualizations. As AI continues to evolve, we can expect even more innovative data visualization techniques that will unlock the secrets hidden within data and help us make better decisions, solve complex problems, and shape a better future.

Beyond the Visual: The Power of Storytelling

Data visualization is more than just charts and graphs; it's about telling stories with data. Effective data visualizations not only present information but also create narratives that engage the audience, highlight key insights, and inspire action.

Think of a compelling story: It has a beginning, a middle, and an end. It takes the reader on a journey, building suspense, revealing key characters, and ultimately leaving a lasting impression. Data visualization can do the same. It can tell the story of a company's growth, the evolution of a trend, or the impact of a social issue.

Creating Engaging Data Visualizations

To effectively tell stories with data, consider the following principles:

- **Focus on the Audience:** Who are you trying to reach? What are their interests and needs? Tailor your visualizations to your audience's understanding and engage them with relevant insights.
- **Clear and Concise:** Keep your visualizations simple and focused. Avoid clutter and unnecessary complexity. Use clear labels, titles, and annotations to guide the audience's understanding.
- **Tell a Story:** Structure your visualizations to create a narrative flow. Use visual elements like color, size, and shape to emphasize key points and highlight relationships between data points.
- **Encourage Exploration:** Make your visualizations interactive, allowing users to explore data from different angles, filter information, and delve deeper into specific insights.
- **Data Ethics:** Ensure that your visualizations are accurate, unbiased, and ethically presented. Consider the potential impact of your visualizations and strive for transparency and accountability in your data storytelling.

Data Visualization as a Catalyst for Change

Data visualization can be a powerful tool for promoting understanding, driving change, and inspiring action. By transforming data into compelling narratives, we can:

- **Raise Awareness:** Visualize data about social issues, environmental challenges, or global trends to raise awareness and promote understanding of complex problems.
- **Influence Policy:** Use data visualizations to highlight key insights and trends that can inform policy decisions, shape public opinion, and drive change.
- **Inspire Action:** Create visualizations that empower individuals to take action, make informed choices, and contribute to solutions for pressing problems.

As we enter an era of data-driven decision-making, data visualization plays an increasingly critical role in shaping our understanding of the world and guiding our actions. AI is revolutionizing the field, providing us with tools and techniques to create more insightful, engaging, and actionable visualizations. By embracing these tools and embracing the power of data storytelling, we can unlock the secrets hidden within data and create a brighter future for all.

THE ETHICS OF DATA

The vast amounts of data collected and analyzed by AI systems raise crucial ethical questions about privacy, bias, and responsible use. These ethical considerations are paramount in ensuring that AI technology is developed and deployed for the betterment of society.

- **Privacy Concerns:** One of the most significant ethical challenges posed by big data is the issue of privacy. AI systems often require access to vast amounts of personal data, including sensitive information like medical records, financial transactions, and online activity. This raises concerns about the potential misuse of this data, such as identity theft, discrimination, or unauthorized surveillance.
- **Data Collection and Consent:** It is crucial to obtain informed consent from individuals before collecting their data and to ensure that the data is collected ethically and transparently. This includes clearly explaining how the data will be used, who will have access to it, and what security measures are in place to protect it.
- **Data Minimization:** Only the necessary data should be collected, and data should not be retained for longer than is required for the intended purpose. This minimizes the potential for misuse and protects individuals' privacy.
- **Anonymization and Pseudonymization:** Techniques such as anonymization and pseudonymization can be employed to remove or disguise identifiable information from datasets, thereby reducing the risk of privacy violations.

Bias in AI

Another critical ethical challenge is the potential for bias in AI systems. AI algorithms are trained on data, and if that data contains biases, the AI system may learn and perpetuate those biases. This can have serious consequences, leading to discriminatory outcomes in various areas, such as loan approvals, hiring decisions, and criminal justice.

- **Data Bias:** Bias can be present in the data used to train AI systems due to historical inequalities, societal prejudices, or sampling errors. For example, training an AI system for facial recognition on datasets that primarily feature white faces may lead to inaccurate results for people of color.
- **Algorithmic Bias:** Bias can also arise from the design and implementation of AI algorithms themselves. Certain algorithms may be more susceptible to bias than others, and even seemingly neutral algorithms can produce biased outputs if trained on biased data.

Mitigating Bias

Addressing bias in AI requires a multi-pronged approach:

- **Data Diversity:** Ensuring that the data used to train AI systems is diverse and representative of the population it will be used on is crucial. This means collecting data from a variety of sources and perspectives to reduce the impact of historical bias.
- **Algorithmic Fairness:** Developing and using algorithms that are designed to be fair and unbiased is also essential. This may involve incorporating fairness

metrics into the algorithm's design or using techniques to mitigate bias during training.

- **Transparency and Accountability:** Transparency and accountability are critical in addressing bias. Making the data and algorithms used in AI systems more transparent allows for scrutiny and helps identify and mitigate potential biases.

Responsible Use of AI

The ethical use of AI extends beyond privacy and bias. It is crucial to consider the broader societal implications of AI and ensure that it is used responsibly and ethically.

- **Social Impact Assessment:** Before deploying AI systems, it is essential to conduct a thorough social impact assessment to understand the potential positive and negative consequences of the technology. This includes assessing the impact on employment, social equity, and environmental sustainability.
- **Ethical Guidelines and Regulations:** Developing and enforcing ethical guidelines and regulations for the development and deployment of AI is essential to ensure that the technology is used for good and not for harm. These guidelines should address issues such as data privacy, bias, transparency, and accountability.
- **Public Engagement:** Engaging the public in discussions about the ethical implications of AI is crucial to ensure that the technology is developed and used in a way that aligns with societal values. This can involve public forums, workshops, and educational

programs to raise awareness and foster informed debate.

CONCLUSION

As AI continues to evolve and become increasingly integrated into our lives, it is essential to address the ethical challenges associated with big data. Navigating privacy concerns, mitigating bias, and ensuring responsible data practices in AI is crucial to harnessing the transformative power of AI for the benefit of all. By prioritizing ethical considerations in AI development and deployment, we can help ensure that AI technology is used for good and contributes to a more just and equitable future.

CHAPTER 3

THE BRAINS BEHIND THE MACHINE

MACHINE LEARNING

Imagine a world where computers can learn and adapt like humans, gleaning insights from vast amounts of data to solve complex problems, make predictions, and even create art. This is the realm of machine learning, a powerful subset of artificial intelligence (AI) that empowers machines to learn from experience without explicit programming.

Machine learning is the brain behind AI's ability to recognize patterns, make decisions, and generate new ideas. It's the force that allows self-driving cars to navigate roads, facial recognition systems to identify individuals, and spam filters to keep our inboxes clean.

At its core, machine learning is about building algorithms that can learn from data. These algorithms are not explicitly programmed to perform specific tasks; instead, they are trained on massive datasets to identify patterns and relationships. Think of it like teaching a child to recognize a dog. You wouldn't give them a list of specific instructions; instead, you'd show them pictures of dogs, pointing out their key features and helping them learn to identify them independently.

Machine learning algorithms fall into several categories, each with its own unique approach to learning from data:

1. **Supervised Learning:** This is like having a teacher who provides labeled examples for the algorithm to learn from. Imagine you want to teach a machine to distinguish between pictures of cats and dogs. You would provide labeled examples—pictures of cats labeled "cat" and pictures of dogs labeled "dog"—and the algorithm would learn to associate specific features with each label. Once trained, the algorithm can then classify new, unseen pictures, predicting whether they contain a cat or a dog.
   - **Common supervised learning algorithms include:**
   - **Linear Regression:** Used to predict continuous values, like predicting the price of a house based on its size and location.
   - **Logistic Regression:** Used to predict categorical values, like predicting whether a customer will buy a product or not.
   - **Support Vector Machines (SVMs):** Used for classification tasks, like classifying emails as spam or not spam.
   - **Decision Trees:** Used for both classification and regression tasks, creating a hierarchical tree structure to make predictions.

2. **Unsupervised Learning:** In this scenario, the algorithm learns from unlabeled data, uncovering hidden patterns and structures without explicit guidance. Imagine you have a dataset of customer purchase history without any labels. Unsupervised learning algorithms can analyze this data to group customers based on their purchasing habits, discovering valuable insights about their preferences and behaviors.

   - **Common unsupervised learning algorithms include:**
   - **Clustering:** Groups data points into clusters based on their similarity, like grouping customers into different segments based on their purchasing patterns.
   - **Dimensionality Reduction:** Reduces the number of variables in a dataset while preserving the most important information, like finding the most relevant features that influence customer satisfaction.
   - **Association Rule Mining:** Discovers relationships between different items in a dataset, like finding out that customers who buy milk also often buy bread.

3. **Reinforcement Learning:** This is like teaching a child to ride a bicycle by rewarding them for staying balanced and penalizing them for falling. Reinforcement learning algorithms learn through trial and error, receiving feedback from the environment in the form of rewards or punishments. The goal is to optimize the algorithm's behavior to maximize rewards over time.

   - **Common reinforcement learning algorithms include:**

- **Q-learning:** Used for learning optimal actions in sequential decision-making problems, like teaching a robot to navigate a maze.
- **Deep Reinforcement Learning:** Combines reinforcement learning with deep neural networks, enabling the learning of complex and sophisticated strategies, like playing video games at a superhuman level.

Machine Learning: A Revolution in Progress

Machine learning is transforming industries across the globe, from healthcare to finance to manufacturing. It is powering innovations that were once thought impossible, like diagnosing diseases with greater accuracy, predicting market trends with precision, and creating personalized learning experiences.

Here are some real-world examples of how machine learning is making a difference:

- **Healthcare:** Machine learning is revolutionizing disease diagnosis, treatment, and drug discovery. Algorithms can analyze medical images to detect abnormalities, predict patient outcomes, and personalize treatment plans.
- **Finance:** Machine learning is being used to optimize investments, detect fraud, and improve risk management. Algorithms can analyze financial data to identify patterns, predict market trends, and make informed investment decisions.
- **Transportation:** Machine learning is driving the development of self-driving cars, traffic management systems, and other intelligent transportation

technologies. Algorithms can analyze sensor data to navigate roads, optimize traffic flow, and enhance safety.

- **Education:** Machine learning is being used to personalize learning, adapt to students' individual needs, and improve educational outcomes. Algorithms can analyze student data to create custom learning paths, provide tailored feedback, and identify areas for improvement.

Machine learning is still a rapidly evolving field, with new algorithms and applications emerging all the time. However, one thing is certain: machine learning is transforming the world around us, opening up new possibilities and shaping the future in profound ways.

Ethical Considerations in Machine Learning

As machine learning becomes more sophisticated, it is crucial to address the ethical considerations that arise from its use. Here are some key issues:

- **Bias:** Machine learning algorithms can inherit biases from the data they are trained on. If the training data reflects societal biases, the algorithm may perpetuate those biases in its predictions, leading to unfair outcomes.
- **Privacy:** Machine learning often involves collecting and analyzing sensitive personal data. It is crucial to ensure that this data is collected and used responsibly, respecting individuals' privacy and security.
- **Job Displacement:** As machine learning automates tasks, there is a concern about job displacement. It is

important to consider how to prepare for this potential shift in the labor market, promoting reskilling and upskilling to equip workers for the jobs of the future.

- **Transparency:** Machine learning algorithms can be complex and opaque, making it difficult to understand how they reach their decisions. It is important to develop techniques for making these algorithms more transparent, enabling humans to understand and trust their outputs.

The Future of Machine Learning

Machine learning is poised to continue its transformative journey, with advancements in areas like deep learning, reinforcement learning, and natural language processing. The future holds exciting possibilities for AI-powered innovations that can solve complex problems, improve our lives, and create a more sustainable and equitable future.

Here are some key trends shaping the future of machine learning:

- **Deep Learning:** Deep neural networks, inspired by the structure of the human brain, are becoming increasingly sophisticated, enabling AI to learn from massive datasets and perform complex tasks like natural language understanding and image recognition with unprecedented accuracy.
- **Reinforcement Learning:** Reinforcement learning algorithms are being used to develop AI systems that can learn to adapt to changing environments, optimize their actions over time, and make decisions in complex situations.

- **Natural Language Processing:** AI systems are becoming increasingly adept at understanding and generating human language, enabling applications like automated customer service, personalized language translation, and AI-powered writing assistants.
- **AI for Social Good:** There is growing focus on using AI to address global challenges, such as climate change, poverty, and disease. AI-powered solutions are being developed to monitor environmental changes, predict disease outbreaks, and improve the distribution of resources.

Embracing the Future of Machine Learning

Machine learning is a powerful force shaping our future. By understanding its fundamentals, exploring its applications, and addressing its ethical considerations, we can harness its potential for good, creating a world where technology empowers humanity and drives progress.

As you continue your journey into the world of AI, remember that machine learning is not just about algorithms and data; it's about understanding the human experience, solving problems that matter, and building a better future for all.

Supervised Learning

Imagine a world where computers can learn from experience, just like humans. That's the realm of supervised learning, a fundamental pillar of artificial intelligence (AI). In supervised learning, AI algorithms are trained on labeled datasets, akin to a student learning from a textbook filled with annotated examples. Each piece of data in the training set is carefully paired with its corresponding label, providing the AI with a clear understanding of what it's supposed to learn.

Think of it like teaching a child to identify different fruits. You show them a picture of an apple and say, "This is an apple." You then repeat this process with various fruits, associating each image with its correct name. Over time, the child learns to recognize the different fruits based on their visual features.

Supervised learning works similarly. The labeled dataset acts as the "textbook," providing the AI with examples and their associated labels. The AI algorithm, like a curious student, analyzes these examples, seeking to understand the relationships between the data and the labels. This process is called training.

During training, the AI algorithm adjusts its internal parameters, essentially tweaking its understanding of the data and labels. The goal is to develop a model that can accurately predict or classify new, unseen data based on the knowledge gained from the training set.

Types of Supervised Learning

Supervised learning is broadly categorized into two main types:

- **Regression:** This type of learning focuses on predicting continuous values, like the price of a house or the temperature tomorrow. The AI algorithm learns a relationship between the input data and the continuous output variable.
- **Classification:** This type of learning aims to categorize data into distinct classes, like identifying spam emails or classifying images of different animals. The AI algorithm learns to assign input data to specific

categories based on the provided labels.

Supervised Learning in Action

Let's delve into some real-world applications of supervised learning to understand its power and versatility:

- **Image Recognition:** Imagine an app that automatically identifies different breeds of dogs. Supervised learning enables this capability by training an AI model on a dataset of dog images, each labeled with its corresponding breed. Once trained, the model can analyze new images and predict the breed with high accuracy.
- **Spam Detection:** Email providers employ supervised learning to filter spam emails from your inbox. Training data consists of labeled emails, with spam messages marked as such. The AI algorithm learns the patterns and characteristics of spam emails, enabling it to identify and filter out new spam messages.
- **Medical Diagnosis:** AI algorithms are being used to assist doctors in diagnosing diseases. Supervised learning plays a crucial role by training models on medical images, patient records, and other medical data. These models can analyze new data and provide insights that support diagnostic decisions, potentially leading to faster and more accurate diagnosis.
- **Financial Forecasting:** Supervised learning is used to predict stock prices, analyze financial trends, and detect potential fraud. AI algorithms are trained on historical financial data, enabling them to identify patterns and make predictions about future financial movements.

The Importance of Labeled Data

The success of supervised learning hinges on the quality and quantity of labeled data. If the data is inaccurate, incomplete, or biased, the AI model will learn flawed patterns and produce inaccurate predictions.

Therefore, meticulous data collection, cleaning, and labeling are essential steps in developing reliable supervised learning models. This process involves ensuring that the data is representative of the real-world scenarios the AI will encounter and that the labels are accurate and consistent.

Challenges and Limitations of Supervised Learning

Despite its impressive capabilities, supervised learning faces certain challenges and limitations:

- **Data Dependence:** Supervised learning heavily relies on the availability of large, labeled datasets. Acquiring and labeling such data can be time-consuming and expensive, especially in specialized domains.
- **Overfitting:** Overfitting occurs when the AI model becomes too specialized in the training data and fails to generalize well to new, unseen data. This can lead to inaccurate predictions in real-world applications.
- **Bias:** The training data can reflect existing biases present in the real world, which can be amplified by the AI model. This can lead to unfair or discriminatory outcomes, highlighting the importance of ensuring data fairness and ethical considerations in AI development.

Conclusion

Supervised learning represents a powerful paradigm in AI, enabling computers to learn from labeled data and make predictions or classifications. By understanding the principles of supervised learning, its applications, and its limitations, we can better appreciate its potential to revolutionize various industries and aspects of our lives. However, it's crucial to approach AI development responsibly, addressing ethical concerns and ensuring data fairness to harness the true potential of supervised learning for the betterment of society.

Unsupervised Learning

Imagine you have a vast collection of photos, but you haven't labeled them. It's a jumble of images—landscapes, portraits, animals, objects—a chaotic mix of visual information. How can you organize this unlabeled collection and find hidden connections between the images? This is where unsupervised learning steps in, a powerful technique in AI that allows algorithms to explore data without explicit instructions, discovering hidden patterns and structures within unlabeled datasets.

In contrast to supervised learning, where AI models are trained on labeled data, unsupervised learning delves into the world of uncharted territories, finding order and structure in seemingly random information. It's like a detective who sifts through clues, uncovering hidden connections and revealing insights that were previously obscured.

One of the fundamental tasks in unsupervised learning is clustering. It's akin to grouping similar items together—like sorting your clothes by color, or organizing books by genre. In clustering, AI algorithms analyze the data points and identify groups based on shared characteristics or similarities. Imagine grouping your unlabeled photos based on their colors, objects, or even the overall theme of the image. This grouping process can be achieved through various clustering algorithms like k-means, hierarchical clustering, and density-based clustering, each with its own strengths and approaches to finding the optimal grouping.

Imagine a large dataset of customer purchase histories. An unsupervised learning algorithm can analyze this data and identify distinct customer segments based on their purchasing patterns. For example, it might uncover groups of customers who regularly buy organic food, a group who primarily purchases electronics, and another group who focuses on clothing. This segmentation can be valuable for businesses as they tailor their marketing campaigns and product recommendations to different customer groups.

Another key application of unsupervised learning is anomaly detection, which involves identifying unusual or outlier data points. Think of a security system that constantly monitors a network for suspicious activity. An anomaly detection algorithm can analyze network traffic and flag any patterns that deviate significantly from the norm, potentially signaling a security breach. This technique can be used in various domains, from fraud detection in financial transactions to medical diagnosis, where identifying unusual patterns can be crucial for early detection and intervention.

Dimensionality reduction is another powerful technique in unsupervised learning that simplifies complex datasets by reducing the number of variables while preserving essential information. Think of a map that condenses a vast geographic space onto a smaller surface while still representing the relative positions of cities and landmarks. Dimensionality reduction algorithms like principal component analysis (PCA) and t-SNE can similarly condense high-dimensional data into lower-dimensional representations, making it easier to visualize and analyze. This technique is particularly valuable when dealing with large datasets, where the complexity of the data can overwhelm traditional analysis methods.

While unsupervised learning excels at uncovering hidden patterns and structures in data, it also comes with certain challenges. One common issue is determining the optimal number of clusters or the appropriate criteria for identifying anomalies. This can be subjective and require careful consideration of the specific dataset and application. Additionally, interpreting the patterns and insights discovered through unsupervised learning can be complex and require domain expertise to ensure meaningful conclusions.

Despite these challenges, unsupervised learning holds immense potential across a wide range of applications. It's a powerful tool for exploring uncharted territories in data, uncovering hidden gems, and driving deeper understanding of complex phenomena. As AI continues to evolve, unsupervised learning is poised to play a pivotal role in unlocking new discoveries, driving innovation, and transforming our understanding of the world around us.

Let's explore a few real-world applications of unsupervised learning:

- **Customer segmentation:** Unsupervised learning can be used to group customers based on their purchasing behavior, demographics, and other characteristics, helping businesses target their marketing efforts more effectively.
- **Image recognition:** Unsupervised learning algorithms can be used to cluster images based on visual features, enabling image recognition systems to categorize images without manual labeling.
- **Fraud detection:** By identifying unusual patterns in financial transactions, unsupervised learning can help detect fraudulent activity and prevent financial losses.
- **Medical diagnosis:** Unsupervised learning can be used to analyze medical images and patient data, aiding in the early detection of diseases and improving diagnostic accuracy.
- **Recommendation systems:** Unsupervised learning algorithms can analyze user preferences and behavior to recommend products, movies, and other content tailored to individual tastes.
- **Data cleaning:** Unsupervised learning can be used to identify and remove outliers and inconsistencies in data, improving data quality and reliability for downstream analysis.

Here are some examples of popular unsupervised learning algorithms:

- **K-means clustering:** This algorithm partitions data points into a predefined number of clusters, minimizing the distance between each data point and its assigned cluster center. It's like organizing your photos into folders, with each folder representing a different cluster.

- **Hierarchical clustering:** This algorithm creates a hierarchical tree-like structure that represents the relationships between data points. It's like organizing your photos into a nested hierarchy, with subfolders within folders, reflecting the varying degrees of similarity between images.
- **Density-based clustering:** This algorithm identifies clusters based on the density of data points in the space. It's like identifying clusters of photos based on their proximity to each other—dense clusters represent groups of similar images, while sparse areas indicate outliers.
- **Principal component analysis (PCA):** This technique reduces the dimensionality of data by finding principal components that capture the most variance in the dataset. It's like summarizing a large dataset into a smaller set of key features, making it easier to understand and visualize.
- **t-SNE:** This algorithm reduces the dimensionality of data while preserving the local neighborhood structure. It's like creating a map that accurately represents the relative positions of cities and landmarks, even though it's a simplified representation of the actual geographic space.

Understanding the different types of unsupervised learning algorithms is crucial for selecting the most appropriate approach for a given task. Each algorithm has its own strengths and weaknesses, and its effectiveness depends on the specific characteristics of the dataset and the objectives of the analysis.

For instance:

- **K-means clustering** is well-suited for datasets with clear and well-defined clusters.
- **Hierarchical clustering** is useful when the number of clusters is unknown or when you want to explore the relationships between data points at different levels of granularity.
- **Density-based clustering** excels at identifying clusters with irregular shapes or varying densities.
- **PCA** is a powerful tool for data visualization and dimensionality reduction in high-dimensional datasets.
- **t-SNE** is particularly effective for visualizing complex relationships in high-dimensional data, especially when the data is non-linear.

The power of unsupervised learning lies in its ability to extract meaningful insights from unlabeled data, revealing patterns and structures that might otherwise be hidden. By applying the right techniques and understanding the nuances of different algorithms, we can unlock the potential of unsupervised learning to uncover new discoveries, drive innovation, and shape a future where AI empowers humanity.

REINFORCEMENT LEARNING

Imagine a young child learning to ride a bicycle. At first, they stumble and fall, their efforts met with frustration. But with each attempt, they receive feedback from the environment – the feeling of wobbly wheels, the scrapes on their knees, the encouragement from their parents. Gradually, they learn to balance, steer, and pedal, eventually mastering the art of cycling. This, in essence, is the core principle of reinforcement learning, a powerful branch of AI that empowers machines to learn through trial and error, just like our little cyclist.

Reinforcement learning is like training a dog with treats and scoldings. The AI agent, like the dog, is presented with a task or a goal. It interacts with its environment, performing actions and observing the consequences. If the action results in a positive outcome, the AI receives a "reward," encouraging it to repeat that action in the future. Conversely, if the action leads to a negative outcome, the AI receives a "punishment," prompting it to avoid that action. Through this continuous feedback loop of rewards and punishments, the AI agent learns to optimize its behavior and achieve its goals.

One of the most compelling aspects of reinforcement learning is its ability to handle complex tasks that are difficult or impossible to program explicitly. This is where its strength lies. Unlike supervised learning, which requires labeled data to train AI models, reinforcement learning allows the AI to learn from its own experiences, even in environments where the optimal solution is unknown. This makes it particularly well-suited for scenarios involving real-world applications, where complex dynamics and uncertainties exist.

Let's consider a few compelling examples:

- **Gaming:** Reinforcement learning has revolutionized the gaming industry. AI agents have been trained to play games like chess, Go, and even video games, achieving superhuman levels of performance. By playing countless games against themselves, these AI agents learn to anticipate opponent moves, develop winning strategies, and adapt to changing game dynamics.

- **Robotics:** In robotics, reinforcement learning is used to train robots to perform complex tasks, such as grasping objects, navigating obstacles, and assembling products. Imagine a robot tasked with assembling a car. It may initially struggle to grasp the correct parts or place them in the right positions. Through reinforcement learning, the robot learns to optimize its movements, identify optimal grasping points, and adjust its actions based on feedback from the environment – the physical world it interacts with.

- **Finance:** In finance, reinforcement learning is used to optimize investment strategies. AI agents can analyze vast amounts of financial data and identify patterns that predict market trends. By simulating different investment scenarios, the AI agent learns to make decisions that maximize returns while minimizing risks.

- **Healthcare:** In healthcare, reinforcement learning is being used to develop personalized treatment plans for patients. AI agents can analyze patient data, such as medical history, genetic information, and medication response, to determine the best course of treatment for each individual. By monitoring patient outcomes and adjusting treatment plans based on feedback, these AI systems can continuously improve their effectiveness and personalize care.

However, reinforcement learning is not without its challenges. One major hurdle is the design of effective reward functions. The choice of rewards can significantly influence the AI agent's behavior and determine whether it achieves its goals. An ill-defined reward function can lead the AI to develop unexpected and undesirable behaviors, potentially leading to unintended consequences.

Another challenge lies in the exploration-exploitation dilemma. The AI agent must balance exploring new actions to discover potentially better solutions with exploiting its current knowledge to maximize its reward. Striking the right balance between exploration and exploitation is crucial for ensuring that the AI agent learns efficiently and effectively.

Furthermore, reinforcement learning algorithms often require a significant amount of data and computational resources to train effectively. In some cases, it may take the AI agent a considerable amount of time and effort to learn a new task, especially if the environment is complex. This can pose a challenge in time-sensitive situations where immediate results are required.

Despite these challenges, reinforcement learning holds immense potential for solving complex problems in various domains. As AI technology continues to evolve, reinforcement learning is likely to play an increasingly prominent role in shaping the future of artificial intelligence. It has the potential to enable AI agents to learn and adapt in real-world environments, where traditional AI approaches struggle. This opens up a world of possibilities for automating tasks, improving decision-making, and creating novel solutions to complex problems.

However, it is important to remember that reinforcement learning is not a magic bullet. It is a powerful tool that requires careful design, implementation, and evaluation. We must be mindful of its limitations and potential biases, and we must ensure that it is used responsibly and ethically. The future of AI lies not in replacing human intelligence but in augmenting it, and reinforcement learning holds the key to unlocking this potential.

As we delve deeper into the fascinating world of reinforcement learning, we'll explore its key concepts, algorithms, and applications in greater detail. We'll uncover the intricacies of training AI agents, designing effective reward functions, and navigating the challenges of exploration and exploitation. We'll also examine the ethical considerations that arise from the use of reinforcement learning and discuss its potential impact on society.

By understanding the principles behind reinforcement learning, we can harness its power for good, creating a future where AI empowers humanity to achieve its full potential. The journey into reinforcement learning begins now. Are you ready to embark on this exciting adventure?

The Future of Machine Learning

The future of machine learning is brimming with exciting possibilities, pushing the boundaries of what AI can achieve. We are witnessing a rapid evolution in this field, fueled by advancements in computing power, data availability, and algorithmic innovation. These advancements are opening up new frontiers in AI capabilities, ushering in a transformative era across various industries and aspects of human life.

One of the most prominent trends shaping the future of machine learning is the rise of **deep learning**. This subfield of machine learning involves the use of artificial neural networks, complex structures inspired by the human brain's architecture. Deep learning models excel in tasks involving complex patterns recognition, such as image and speech recognition, natural language processing, and even drug discovery. Their ability to process vast amounts of data and extract meaningful insights has revolutionized fields like computer vision, natural language processing, and medical diagnostics.

The development of **generative adversarial networks (GANs)** is another significant advancement. GANs consist of two competing neural networks: a generator that creates synthetic data and a discriminator that distinguishes real from fake data. This adversarial setup leads to a continuous improvement process, where the generator learns to create increasingly realistic data, while the discriminator becomes better at detecting fakes. GANs have demonstrated remarkable capabilities in generating high-fidelity images, videos, and even text, opening up possibilities in areas like art creation, content generation, and data augmentation.

Reinforcement learning (RL) is another area experiencing rapid progress. RL algorithms learn through trial and error, optimizing their behavior based on feedback from the environment. This learning paradigm has proven highly effective in automating complex tasks, such as playing games, controlling robots, and even optimizing financial trading strategies. As RL algorithms become more sophisticated, we can expect them to play an increasingly prominent role in automating tasks across various domains.

Beyond these specific advancements, the future of machine learning is characterized by a **convergence of disciplines**, blurring the lines between AI, computer science, and other fields. We see AI techniques being integrated into fields like biology, chemistry, and even social sciences, leading to novel applications and breakthroughs. For example, AI is being used to analyze biological data, predict protein structures, and even design new drugs, revolutionizing the field of medicine.

However, as AI capabilities continue to expand, we must address **ethical considerations** with increasing urgency. Issues related to data privacy, bias, and job displacement require careful attention and proactive solutions. Ensuring that AI is developed and deployed responsibly is crucial to harnessing its potential for good while minimizing risks to society.

The future of machine learning is not just about pushing the boundaries of technological capabilities; it is also about ensuring that these advancements are used for the benefit of humanity. As AI becomes more sophisticated, it becomes essential to develop a framework for ethical AI development and deployment, ensuring that AI systems are aligned with human values and goals.

The future holds immense potential for AI to revolutionize the way we live, work, and interact with the world. By embracing responsible innovation and fostering collaboration between humans and machines, we can shape a future where AI empowers humanity to overcome challenges, enhance well-being, and unlock new frontiers of discovery.

CHAPTER 4

AI IN ACTION – REVOLUTIONIZING INDUSTRIES

AI IN HEALTHCARE

The healthcare industry is undergoing a monumental transformation, and at the heart of this revolution lies artificial intelligence (AI). AI's ability to analyze vast amounts of data, identify complex patterns, and learn from experience is transforming how we diagnose, treat, and care for patients. From speeding up diagnoses to personalizing treatment plans, AI is poised to revolutionize patient care and enhance outcomes across the healthcare spectrum.

One of the most significant ways AI is impacting healthcare is by improving diagnosis. AI algorithms can analyze medical images like X-rays, CT scans, and MRIs with incredible accuracy, helping doctors identify abnormalities that might be missed by the human eye. Imagine a world where AI-powered tools can detect early signs of cancer, cardiovascular disease, or other life-threatening conditions, allowing for timely intervention and improved treatment outcomes.

AI's ability to analyze patient data, including medical records, genetic information, and even wearable device readings, enables the creation of personalized treatment plans tailored to each individual's unique needs and circumstances. This level of personalization can lead to more effective treatments, reduced side effects, and improved patient outcomes. Imagine a future where AI-powered systems can analyze a patient's genetic makeup to predict their risk of certain diseases, allowing for preventive measures and tailored therapies.

AI is also playing a crucial role in revolutionizing patient care. From chatbots that provide 24/7 support and answer patient questions to virtual assistants that help manage medications and schedule appointments, AI is making healthcare more accessible, convenient, and efficient. Imagine a world where AI-powered robots can assist with surgeries, providing surgeons with enhanced precision and minimizing risks.

AI in Diagnosis: A Revolution in Accuracy and Speed

AI's ability to analyze medical images is revolutionizing diagnostic accuracy and efficiency. Machine learning algorithms trained on vast datasets of medical images can identify subtle patterns and abnormalities that might escape human observation. This capability is particularly valuable in areas like radiology, pathology, and ophthalmology, where accurate interpretation of images is paramount.

For instance, AI-powered tools can assist radiologists in detecting tumors in mammograms, identifying signs of pneumonia in chest X-rays, and even detecting early signs of Alzheimer's disease in brain scans. These applications not only enhance diagnostic accuracy but also speed up the diagnostic process, enabling faster treatment decisions and potentially saving lives.

Personalized Medicine: Tailoring Treatment to the Individual

AI is transforming the practice of medicine from a one-size-fits-all approach to a personalized one. By analyzing patient data, including medical history, genetic information, lifestyle factors, and even social determinants of health, AI can develop treatment plans tailored to each individual's unique needs and circumstances.

One example of AI's impact on personalized medicine is in cancer treatment. AI algorithms can analyze tumor characteristics, patient genetics, and treatment responses to determine the most effective therapies. This personalized approach can lead to better treatment outcomes, fewer side effects, and improved quality of life for cancer patients.

Revolutionizing Patient Care: Enhanced Accessibility and Efficiency

AI is not only transforming diagnosis and treatment but also revolutionizing patient care. AI-powered chatbots and virtual assistants are transforming the way patients interact with healthcare providers. These intelligent systems can answer patient questions, schedule appointments, manage medications, and even provide personalized health recommendations.

Imagine a world where patients can interact with AI-powered chatbots for basic healthcare needs, freeing up human healthcare professionals to focus on more complex tasks. This enhanced accessibility can significantly improve patient satisfaction and reduce wait times, making healthcare more convenient and accessible to everyone.

The Future of AI in Healthcare: Unleashing a New Era of Innovation

The impact of AI in healthcare is just beginning to unfold. As AI technologies continue to evolve and mature, we can expect even more groundbreaking applications and innovations. Imagine a future where:

- **AI-powered robots assist with surgeries, enhancing precision and minimizing risks.**
- **AI-powered devices monitor patients' vital signs in real time, alerting doctors to potential problems before they become serious.**
- **AI algorithms analyze patient data to identify early signs of disease, allowing for preventive measures and early interventions.**
- **AI-powered systems develop personalized drug therapies tailored to each individual's genetic makeup and medical history.**

The future of healthcare with AI is brimming with exciting possibilities, promising a future where we can diagnose diseases more accurately, treat patients more effectively, and care for them more efficiently than ever before.

The Ethical Landscape: Addressing the Challenges of AI in Healthcare

While the potential of AI in healthcare is undeniable, it's crucial to address the ethical challenges and considerations that arise with its use. These include:

Bias in AI: Mitigating Unfair Outcomes

AI algorithms are only as good as the data they are trained on. If the training data is biased, the resulting AI system can perpetuate those biases, leading to unfair or discriminatory outcomes. For instance, an AI system trained on medical data that is predominantly from white males might not be able to accurately diagnose or treat patients from other demographic groups. It is imperative to ensure that AI systems are trained on diverse and representative datasets to mitigate biases and ensure fair and equitable outcomes for all patients.

Privacy and Security: Protecting Patient Data

AI in healthcare relies heavily on patient data, including sensitive medical information. It is essential to ensure the privacy and security of this data to protect patient confidentiality and prevent unauthorized access. Robust data security measures, including encryption, access controls, and data anonymization, are crucial to safeguarding patient information.

AI and the Future of Work: Reskilling and Upskilling in a Changing Job Market

The adoption of AI in healthcare has raised concerns about job displacement. While AI is automating some tasks, it is also creating new opportunities and transforming existing roles. Healthcare professionals will need to adapt to this changing landscape by acquiring new skills and embracing the potential of AI as a valuable tool.

The Human-AI Partnership: Collaborating for a Better Future

The future of healthcare is not about AI replacing humans but rather about AI augmenting human capabilities and empowering healthcare professionals to provide better care. AI can be a powerful tool to enhance diagnostic accuracy, personalize treatment plans, and streamline patient care processes. However, it is vital to remember that AI should be used as a tool to support, augment, and enhance human expertise, not to replace it. The future of healthcare lies in a collaborative partnership between humans and AI, working together to unlock the full potential of technology for the benefit of patients.

Embracing the N.E.R.D.Y. Way: A Call to Action

The world of AI is constantly evolving, and it is crucial to stay informed about the latest advancements, potential applications, and ethical considerations. Embrace the N.E.R.D.Y. Way - a journey of knowledge, education, resourcefulness, discovery, and engagement with the world of AI. Get involved in the AI community, explore online resources, and contribute to the responsible development and deployment of AI in healthcare. By understanding AI, its capabilities, and its limitations, we can shape its future and ensure it benefits humanity.

The future of healthcare is bright with the promise of AI. As we embrace this technological revolution, we must strive for responsible innovation, ethical development, and a collaborative partnership between humans and AI. Together, we can unlock the full potential of AI to improve healthcare for all.

AI in Finance

Imagine a world where financial decisions are no longer driven by intuition or guesswork, but by the cold, hard logic of artificial intelligence. This is the reality that AI is bringing to the realm of finance, revolutionizing how we invest, manage risk, and protect our financial well-being. AI algorithms, trained on vast datasets of financial data, are transforming the financial landscape, offering a range of benefits that were once unimaginable.

AI-Powered Investment Strategies

Gone are the days of relying solely on human analysts to sift through mountains of data, searching for investment opportunities. AI is now taking center stage, employing machine learning algorithms to analyze market trends, predict stock prices, and identify potential investment opportunities with unprecedented accuracy. These algorithms are not bound by human biases or emotions, allowing them to analyze data objectively and identify patterns that may escape human perception.

One key area where AI is making a significant impact is in **algorithmic trading**, where computer programs execute trades automatically based on pre-defined rules. This allows for faster, more efficient execution of trades, eliminating human error and emotional influences. AI-powered trading platforms can analyze market data in real-time, identifying fleeting opportunities and executing trades at optimal times, maximizing returns and minimizing risks.

But AI's influence extends beyond trading. **Robo-advisors**, AI-powered platforms that provide automated investment advice, are gaining popularity among investors of all levels. These advisors leverage AI to create personalized investment portfolios based on individual risk tolerance, financial goals, and investment time horizons. Robo-advisors offer cost-effective and accessible investment solutions, particularly for those who may not have the resources to hire a traditional financial advisor.

AI as a Fraud Detection Shield

The financial world is constantly under threat from fraudsters, who employ sophisticated tactics to exploit vulnerabilities and siphon off valuable funds. Traditional fraud detection methods often struggle to keep pace with evolving fraud schemes, leading to significant financial losses. However, AI is emerging as a formidable weapon against financial crime, providing a powerful tool to detect and prevent fraud.

AI algorithms can analyze vast amounts of data, identifying patterns and anomalies that might indicate fraudulent activity. These algorithms can learn to recognize common fraud patterns, such as unusual spending habits, multiple account access attempts from different locations, or suspicious transactions occurring outside typical timeframes. By analyzing transactional data, AI can flag suspicious activities and trigger alerts, allowing financial institutions to intervene and prevent fraud.

Enhancing Cybersecurity with AI

The digital landscape is a battleground for cybercriminals, who constantly seek to breach security systems and steal sensitive data. Traditional cybersecurity measures, while effective in some cases, struggle to keep up with the increasing sophistication of cyberattacks. AI is stepping in to bolster cybersecurity defenses, providing an intelligent shield against these threats.

AI algorithms can analyze network traffic patterns, identifying anomalies that could signal a cyberattack. These algorithms can also be used to detect malicious code in software and emails, preventing malware from infiltrating systems. Moreover, AI can be used to monitor user behavior and identify suspicious activity, such as unauthorized access attempts or unusual data access patterns.

AI's Impact on Financial Security

The financial industry is embracing AI not only to detect fraud and enhance security but also to protect its own systems from cyberattacks. AI-powered security solutions are used to monitor network activity, detect suspicious traffic patterns, and identify potential threats in real-time. These systems can learn from past cyberattacks, constantly adapting and improving their defenses to stay ahead of emerging threats.

AI is also being used to improve **identity verification** and authentication processes, reducing the risk of unauthorized access to accounts. By analyzing facial recognition data, voice patterns, and other biometric information, AI can verify user identities with greater accuracy and speed than traditional methods.

The Challenges of AI in Finance

While AI offers significant benefits to the financial industry, it also presents challenges that must be addressed. One major concern is **bias in algorithms**. AI algorithms are trained on data, and if that data reflects historical biases, the algorithms may perpetuate those biases, leading to unfair or discriminatory outcomes. For example, an AI system trained on historical loan approval data may inadvertently perpetuate past biases against certain demographic groups, denying them access to credit unfairly.

Another challenge is **data privacy and security**. AI algorithms rely on vast amounts of data, which raises concerns about data privacy and security. Ensuring that financial data is handled responsibly and securely is crucial to maintaining trust in AI systems.

The Future of AI in Finance

The financial landscape is rapidly transforming as AI continues to advance. In the future, we can expect to see even more sophisticated AI applications in finance, further enhancing investment management, fraud detection, and cybersecurity. AI will play a crucial role in shaping the future of the financial industry, driving innovation and creating new opportunities.

AI's Role in Personal Finance

AI's impact extends beyond large financial institutions, reaching into the lives of individuals. Personalized finance apps are leveraging AI to provide customized financial advice, track expenses, manage budgets, and identify potential savings opportunities. These apps use AI to analyze spending patterns, identify areas where savings can be made, and suggest ways to improve financial habits.

The Future of Human-AI Collaboration

While AI is transforming the financial landscape, it's important to remember that AI is not a replacement for human expertise. Instead, AI should be viewed as a powerful tool that augments human capabilities, allowing us to make better financial decisions and navigate a complex financial world with greater confidence.

The future of finance lies in the collaboration between humans and AI. By leveraging the strengths of both, we can create a more efficient, equitable, and secure financial system for all. AI can analyze data, identify patterns, and provide insights, while human expertise can provide context, judgment, and ethical oversight. This partnership has the potential to unlock new possibilities in finance, leading to a brighter and more prosperous future.

AI IN EDUCATION

The integration of AI into education is a transformative journey that promises to redefine the learning landscape. Imagine a world where students learn at their own pace, guided by personalized learning paths tailored to their unique strengths and weaknesses. This is the promise of AI in education, where technology empowers teachers and empowers students to reach their full potential.

AI-powered learning platforms can analyze student data, identifying their learning styles, knowledge gaps, and areas of interest. These insights enable personalized learning experiences, where students receive customized assignments, adaptive assessments, and targeted support. Imagine a student struggling with a specific math concept. An AI-powered tutor could provide tailored exercises, interactive explanations, and real-time feedback, helping them grasp the challenging concepts and build confidence.

AI can also optimize teaching strategies by providing teachers with valuable insights into student performance and classroom dynamics. Imagine a teacher who receives real-time data on student engagement and understanding during a lesson. This data empowers them to adjust their teaching methods, provide targeted support, and personalize the learning experience for each student. AI can analyze student performance data, identify areas where they need additional support, and recommend specific interventions or resources to address these needs.

The benefits of AI in education extend beyond personalized learning and optimized teaching. AI-powered tools can streamline administrative tasks, freeing up teachers' time to focus on student engagement and instruction. Imagine a system that automates grading, provides real-time feedback, and assists with lesson planning. This not only saves teachers valuable time but also allows them to provide more personalized attention to each student.

AI can enhance student success by providing personalized learning experiences, identifying knowledge gaps, and offering targeted support. It can also help students develop essential skills like critical thinking, problem-solving, and creativity. Imagine a student learning about a historical event through a virtual reality experience powered by AI. This immersive learning experience can bring the past to life, making learning more engaging and memorable.

The use of AI in education is not without its challenges. Concerns about data privacy, potential bias in AI algorithms, and the need to maintain human interaction in the learning process are important considerations. However, by addressing these challenges, AI can revolutionize education, making learning more personalized, engaging, and effective.

The future of education is one where AI empowers teachers and empowers students to thrive. It's a future where students are equipped with the knowledge, skills, and adaptability they need to succeed in an increasingly complex and dynamic world.

Let's delve deeper into some specific examples of how AI is transforming education:

- **Personalized Learning:** AI-powered platforms like Khan Academy and Duolingo analyze student data, identify their learning styles, and create customized learning paths. These platforms provide adaptive assessments, real-time feedback, and personalized recommendations, ensuring students are learning at their own pace and addressing their specific needs.
- **Adaptive Teaching:** Imagine a teacher using an AI-powered tool that provides real-time insights into student engagement and understanding during a lesson. This allows the teacher to adjust their teaching methods, provide targeted support, and personalize the learning experience for each student.
- **Intelligent Tutoring Systems:** AI-powered tutoring systems like Wolfram Alpha and Google Tutor can provide personalized guidance and support to students struggling with specific concepts. These systems offer interactive explanations, tailored exercises, and real-time feedback, helping students master challenging topics.
- **Automated Grading and Feedback:** AI-powered systems can automate the grading process, providing students with instant feedback on their work. This allows teachers to dedicate more time to personalized instruction and support.
- **Student Performance Analysis:** AI can analyze student performance data, identifying areas where they need additional support. This allows teachers to

recommend specific interventions or resources to address these needs.

- **Learning Analytics:** AI-powered learning analytics platforms can track student progress, identify learning patterns, and provide insights into student engagement. These insights empower teachers to tailor their instruction and ensure that students are on track to achieve their learning goals.
- **Virtual Reality and Augmented Reality Learning:** AI-powered virtual reality and augmented reality experiences can create immersive and engaging learning environments. Imagine a student learning about the human body through a VR experience that allows them to explore a virtual anatomical model.
- **AI-Powered Chatbots:** AI-powered chatbots can be used to provide students with 24/7 support and answer their questions about course materials, deadlines, and academic resources.

While AI offers transformative possibilities in education, it's crucial to address the ethical implications and potential challenges:

- **Data Privacy:** Protecting student data is essential, and AI systems must adhere to strict privacy regulations to ensure that sensitive information is not misused.
- **Bias in AI Algorithms:** AI algorithms can inherit biases from the data they are trained on, leading to unfair outcomes. It is crucial to develop AI systems that are fair, unbiased, and equitable for all students.
- **Human Interaction:** While AI can enhance learning, it's important to remember that human interaction is

crucial in education. AI systems should be designed to complement and enhance human interaction, not replace it.

- **Accessibility and Equity:** AI systems should be accessible to all students, regardless of their background or learning needs.

By addressing these challenges and embracing the potential of AI, we can create a future where education is personalized, engaging, and accessible for all.

AI IN MANUFACTURING

Imagine a world where machines not only work alongside humans but also learn and adapt to optimize production processes. This is the reality being shaped by AI in manufacturing, where automation, predictive maintenance, and data-driven insights are revolutionizing the way products are made.

AI's impact on manufacturing extends far beyond mere automation; it's about transforming the entire production ecosystem. Think of it like a symphony orchestra where each instrument, each machine, works in harmony to create a flawless performance – a seamless, efficient, and high-quality product.

4.4: AI in Manufacturing: Automating Processes, Optimizing Production, and Enhancing Efficiency

Automating Repetitive Tasks

AI is automating repetitive tasks, freeing human workers to focus on more complex and creative aspects of their jobs. Robots equipped with AI can perform tasks like welding, assembly, and painting with precision and speed, significantly increasing productivity while minimizing errors. This automation not only improves efficiency but also creates a safer work environment by removing humans from hazardous tasks.

Optimizing Production Processes

AI is optimizing production processes by analyzing vast amounts of data collected from sensors, machines, and other sources. This data provides insights into bottlenecks, inefficiencies, and areas for improvement. AI algorithms can then identify and implement solutions, resulting in faster production times, reduced waste, and increased overall output.

Predictive Maintenance

AI can predict equipment failures before they occur, minimizing downtime and ensuring smooth operations. By analyzing data from sensors that monitor machine performance, AI algorithms can identify patterns that indicate impending failures. This allows for proactive maintenance, preventing costly breakdowns and ensuring consistent production.

Quality Control

AI-powered systems are enhancing quality control by detecting defects that might be missed by human inspectors. AI algorithms can analyze images and videos of products to identify imperfections, ensuring only high-quality products reach consumers.

Enhancing Supply Chain Management

AI is transforming supply chain management by optimizing logistics and forecasting demand. AI algorithms can analyze historical data and real-time information to predict future demand, enabling companies to adjust production accordingly and avoid stockouts or overstocking.

Examples of AI in Manufacturing

- **Automated Guided Vehicles (AGVs):** AGVs are robots equipped with AI that navigate warehouses and factories autonomously, transporting materials and products efficiently.
- **Predictive Maintenance Systems:** AI-powered systems monitor machine performance, identify potential problems, and schedule maintenance before breakdowns occur.
- **AI-Powered Quality Control:** AI algorithms analyze images and videos of products to detect defects and ensure quality.
- **Inventory Optimization Systems:** AI algorithms analyze historical data and real-time information to predict demand and optimize inventory levels.

The Benefits of AI in Manufacturing

The implementation of AI in manufacturing offers numerous benefits, including:

- **Increased Efficiency:** AI automates tasks, streamlines processes, and optimizes production, leading to increased efficiency and productivity.
- **Reduced Costs:** AI reduces waste, minimizes downtime, and optimizes resource allocation, resulting in significant cost savings.
- **Improved Quality:** AI enhances quality control, leading to fewer defects and higher-quality products.

- **Enhanced Safety:** AI removes humans from hazardous tasks, improving worker safety and creating a more secure work environment.
- **Data-Driven Insights:** AI provides valuable insights into production processes, enabling companies to make data-driven decisions for continuous improvement.

Challenges of Implementing AI in Manufacturing

While the potential benefits of AI in manufacturing are significant, there are also challenges to overcome:

- **Data Requirements:** AI algorithms require large amounts of data to learn and perform effectively. This can be a challenge for manufacturers who may not have the necessary data infrastructure or data collection processes in place.
- **Integration Challenges:** Integrating AI systems with existing manufacturing infrastructure can be complex and require significant investment.
- **Skill Gaps:** Implementing and managing AI systems requires specialized skills that may not be readily available in the manufacturing workforce.
- **Ethical Considerations:** The use of AI in manufacturing raises ethical concerns regarding job displacement, privacy, and bias in algorithms.

The Future of AI in Manufacturing

The future of AI in manufacturing is bright, with advancements in AI technologies continuing to drive innovation. Here are some key trends to watch:

- **The Rise of the Smart Factory:** Factories equipped with AI-powered systems that connect and communicate with each other, creating a highly efficient and responsive production environment.
- **Edge AI:** Processing data at the edge of the network, closer to where it is generated, reducing latency and improving real-time decision-making.
- **AI-Powered Robotics:** Robots equipped with AI that can learn and adapt to changing environments, performing tasks with greater flexibility and autonomy.
- **The Convergence of AI and the Industrial Internet of Things (IIoT):** Combining AI with the IIoT to create highly intelligent and connected manufacturing systems.

CONCLUSION

AI is transforming the manufacturing industry, enabling companies to automate processes, optimize production, and enhance efficiency. As AI continues to evolve, its impact on manufacturing will only grow, leading to a future of smarter, more efficient, and more sustainable manufacturing.

AI IN TRANSPORTATION

The realm of transportation is undergoing a profound transformation, with AI at the helm. This revolution isn't just about self-driving cars, though those certainly play a central role. It's about reimagining how we move, how we manage traffic, and how we ensure our safety on the roads.

Autonomous vehicles are the most visible manifestation of AI in transportation. These self-driving cars, trucks, and buses are capable of navigating complex traffic scenarios, adapting to changing conditions, and making decisions that rival, and sometimes surpass, human drivers. The promise of autonomous vehicles is immense: reduced traffic congestion, fewer accidents, and increased accessibility for those who are unable to drive. Imagine a world where your car becomes your personal assistant, taking you safely to your destination while you work, relax, or even sleep. This vision is rapidly becoming reality as automakers and technology giants pour resources into developing and refining autonomous driving technologies.

But autonomous vehicles are just one piece of the AI puzzle. Intelligent traffic management systems are using AI to optimize traffic flow, reducing congestion and delays. These systems leverage real-time data from sensors, cameras, and GPS devices to analyze traffic patterns, predict congestion points, and adjust traffic signals accordingly. The result is a more efficient and fluid transportation network, reducing stress and wasted time for commuters.

AI is also playing a crucial role in enhancing safety on the roads. Advanced driver assistance systems (ADAS) are becoming increasingly sophisticated, incorporating features like lane departure warnings, adaptive cruise control, and emergency braking. These systems use sensors, cameras, and machine learning algorithms to detect potential hazards and assist drivers in avoiding accidents. Furthermore, AI is being employed in the development of safer and more efficient infrastructure, from smart intersections to intelligent road signs that adapt to changing traffic conditions.

The impact of AI on transportation extends beyond the individual driver. AI-powered logistics platforms are transforming the way goods are moved, streamlining delivery routes, optimizing inventory management, and reducing transportation costs. This efficiency translates into lower prices for consumers and a more sustainable supply chain.

However, the integration of AI in transportation is not without its challenges. Ethical considerations surrounding autonomous vehicles, such as liability in the event of an accident, are still being debated. Privacy concerns regarding the collection and use of driver data also need to be addressed. And the potential for job displacement within the transportation industry is a significant social and economic issue that requires careful planning and mitigation strategies.

Looking ahead, the future of transportation with AI is filled with possibilities. We can expect to see increasingly sophisticated autonomous vehicles, capable of navigating even more complex environments and interacting with each other to optimize traffic flow. Intelligent traffic management systems will become more proactive, anticipating traffic needs and seamlessly adjusting to changing conditions. And safety features will continue to advance, utilizing real-time data and machine learning to prevent accidents before they occur.

AI's transformative potential in transportation is undeniable. As technology continues to evolve, it will play an increasingly central role in shaping how we move, how we manage our transportation systems, and how we ensure the safety of all road users. The challenge lies in harnessing this technology responsibly, addressing ethical concerns, and ensuring that the benefits of AI reach every corner of society.

CHAPTER 5

NAVIGATING THE ETHICAL LANDSCAPE

BIAS IN AI

The world of AI is filled with promise and potential, but it also comes with a set of ethical challenges that we must address to ensure that AI benefits all of humanity. One of the most critical issues we face is bias in AI. Bias can creep into AI systems in various ways, leading to unfair outcomes that can perpetuate existing inequalities and even create new ones. This chapter dives into the complex world of bias in AI, exploring the ways it can emerge, its potential consequences, and the strategies we can use to mitigate these issues.

Imagine a hiring system powered by AI that is designed to identify the best candidates for a particular job. This system relies on data from previous hires, analyzing factors like education, experience, and skills to predict the success of future applicants. However, if this data reflects historical hiring practices that were biased against certain groups, the AI system may unwittingly perpetuate those biases. For example, if the historical data shows that men have been hired for a specific role at a higher rate than women, even if their qualifications are similar, the AI system might learn to favor male candidates, leading to an unfair disadvantage for women.

This scenario illustrates a key challenge with AI: its reliance on data. AI systems learn from the data they are trained on, and if that data is biased, the resulting AI system will likely reflect those biases. But bias can emerge not only from the data itself but also from the way the algorithms are designed and implemented. For example, an AI system designed to assess loan applications might use an algorithm that disproportionately favors applicants with higher credit scores, even if those applicants come from privileged backgrounds and are less likely to need a loan in the first place. This type of bias can perpetuate existing financial inequalities, making it harder for people from underrepresented groups to access financial resources.

The consequences of bias in AI can be far-reaching and impactful. They can lead to:

- **Discrimination:** Biased AI systems can lead to unfair discrimination against individuals or groups, based on factors like race, gender, religion, or socioeconomic status. This can manifest in various ways, from biased hiring decisions to unfair access to healthcare or financial services.
- **Amplification of Existing Inequalities:** Biased AI systems can amplify existing societal inequalities by favoring certain groups while disadvantaging others. This can lead to a widening gap between those who benefit from AI and those who are left behind.

- **Erosion of Trust in AI:** When AI systems are perceived as biased or unfair, it can lead to a loss of trust in the technology. This can hinder the adoption of AI and limit its potential to bring positive change.
- **Ethical Concerns:** The presence of bias in AI raises serious ethical concerns about the fairness and trustworthiness of these systems. It challenges us to question the values and assumptions embedded within the algorithms and the data they are trained on.

Recognizing these potential risks is crucial. We must move beyond simply building AI systems and actively work to ensure that these systems are fair, equitable, and unbiased. To address this, we need to develop strategies for mitigating bias throughout the entire AI development lifecycle. This includes:

1. **Data Collection and Preparation:**
   - **Diverse Data:** To mitigate bias, it is crucial to collect data that is representative of the population the AI system is intended to serve. This means collecting data from diverse individuals and groups, ensuring that the data reflects the real-world population as accurately as possible.
   - **Data Quality and Integrity:** The quality and integrity of the data are essential for building unbiased AI systems. This involves identifying and removing any errors, inconsistencies, or outliers in the data that could introduce bias.
   - **Data Augmentation:** Data augmentation techniques can help to increase the diversity and representativeness of the training data, particularly for underrepresented groups. This can involve

creating synthetic data or modifying existing data to ensure that the AI system learns from a wider range of experiences.

2. **Algorithm Design and Training:**
   - **Fairness-Aware Algorithms:** Researchers are developing algorithms specifically designed to be fair and unbiased. These algorithms incorporate measures to detect and mitigate bias, ensuring that the AI system makes fair decisions.
   - **Regularization Techniques:** Regularization techniques can be used during the training process to penalize the AI system for making decisions that are based on protected attributes like race or gender. This helps to discourage the system from learning biased patterns.
   - **Transparency and Explainability:** Transparency in the design and training of AI systems is crucial for understanding and mitigating bias. Explainable AI (XAI) techniques aim to make AI systems more transparent, allowing us to understand how decisions are made and identify any potential sources of bias.

3. **Ongoing Monitoring and Evaluation:**
   - **Continuous Monitoring:** It is essential to continuously monitor AI systems for bias, even after they have been deployed. This involves analyzing the system's performance over time and identifying any emerging patterns of bias.
   - **Auditing and Testing:** Regular audits and testing of AI systems can help to identify and address any potential biases. This might involve evaluating the system's performance on various

datasets or using specialized tools to detect and mitigate bias.

- **Feedback Mechanisms:** Implementing feedback mechanisms to allow users to report any perceived bias in the AI system is crucial. This allows for continuous improvement and helps to ensure that the system remains fair and equitable.

The fight against bias in AI is a continuous effort. It requires collaboration between researchers, developers, policymakers, and the public to ensure that AI technologies are used responsibly and ethically. By actively addressing bias in AI, we can help to create a future where these technologies are used to uplift all of humanity, fostering inclusivity, fairness, and progress for all.

PRIVACY AND SECURITY

Imagine a world where every detail of your life, from your browsing history to your medical records, is meticulously stored and analyzed. This data, often referred to as "sensitive information," holds the potential to unlock incredible insights for both individuals and organizations. Yet, this very same data can also be misused, leading to privacy breaches, discrimination, and other ethical concerns. This is where the critical concept of data privacy and security comes into play.

As AI rapidly advances, its dependence on vast amounts of data becomes increasingly apparent. While this data fuels AI's capabilities and drives innovation, it also presents a Pandora's Box of ethical dilemmas. AI systems, with their ability to analyze and learn from data, inevitably gain access to sensitive information.

This raises crucial questions about how we safeguard our privacy while leveraging AI's power for good.

The ethical implications of AI's access to sensitive information are multifaceted and far-reaching. One pressing concern is the potential for privacy breaches. AI systems often rely on vast datasets, which may include personal information such as medical records, financial data, and even location tracking. If this information falls into the wrong hands, it could lead to identity theft, financial fraud, and other forms of harm.

Another ethical challenge arises from the potential for discrimination. AI algorithms are trained on data, and if this data reflects existing societal biases, the AI systems themselves can become biased. This can lead to unfair outcomes, such as biased hiring practices, discriminatory loan approvals, and even biased criminal justice systems.

The solution to these ethical dilemmas lies in ensuring responsible data management. This involves a multi-pronged approach that combines robust security measures, data privacy regulations, and ethical guidelines for AI development and deployment.

Data Security: A Multi-Layered Defense

Data security is paramount in protecting sensitive information from unauthorized access, alteration, or destruction. This involves implementing a layered security strategy that encompasses physical, technical, and administrative measures.

- **Physical Security:** Ensuring the physical security of data centers and servers is crucial. This includes measures like secure access control, surveillance systems, and environmental monitoring to prevent unauthorized access and physical damage.

- **Technical Security:** Employing strong technical controls is essential to protect data both in transit and at rest. This includes robust encryption methods, secure data storage, and access control mechanisms. Firewalls, intrusion detection systems, and anti-malware software play vital roles in preventing cyberattacks and data breaches.
- **Administrative Security:** Establishing strong administrative controls is equally important. This includes creating clear data security policies, implementing data access protocols, and providing comprehensive training for employees to ensure they understand and adhere to these policies. Regular security audits and vulnerability assessments help identify and address security weaknesses proactively.

Privacy Regulations: Setting the Boundaries

Data privacy regulations aim to protect individuals' personal information and give them control over how their data is collected, used, and shared. These regulations vary across countries and regions, but some common principles include:

- **Notice and Consent:** Individuals should be informed about how their data is being collected, used, and shared. They should also have the opportunity to consent to data processing.
- **Data Minimization:** Only necessary data should be collected and processed.

- **Data Retention:** Data should be retained only for as long as it is needed for the intended purpose.
- **Data Security:** Data should be protected from unauthorized access, alteration, or destruction.
- **Data Subject Rights:** Individuals should have the right to access, correct, erase, and restrict the processing of their data.

Ethical Guidelines: Shaping Responsible AI

Ethical guidelines for AI development and deployment are crucial to ensuring that AI is used responsibly and ethically. These guidelines should address key principles such as:

- **Fairness and Non-discrimination:** AI systems should be designed and developed in a way that does not perpetuate existing societal biases.
- **Transparency and Explainability:** AI systems should be designed to be transparent and explainable, allowing users to understand how decisions are being made.
- **Accountability and Responsibility:** Clear mechanisms should be in place for accountability and responsibility in the development and deployment of AI systems.
- **Data Ownership and Control:** Individuals should have control over their data, including the right to access, modify, or delete it.

The Role of Technology: Enabling Data Privacy and Security

Technological advancements play a crucial role in enhancing data privacy and security. These advancements include:

- **Differential Privacy:** This technique adds noise to data to protect individual privacy while allowing for statistical analysis.
- **Homomorphic Encryption:** This allows data to be processed in encrypted form without decryption, ensuring privacy even during computation.
- **Federated Learning:** This allows AI models to be trained on decentralized data without sharing the data itself, ensuring privacy.
- **Blockchain Technology:** Blockchain provides a secure and transparent ledger for recording data transactions, enhancing data integrity and traceability.

The Importance of Education and Awareness

Educating individuals about data privacy and security is essential for promoting responsible data management. This involves raising awareness about the potential risks of data misuse, empowering individuals to take control of their data, and fostering a culture of data security.

Collaboration and Cooperation: A Shared Responsibility

Building a data-driven future that respects privacy and security requires collaboration and cooperation among governments, businesses, researchers, and individuals. This involves:

- **Government Regulations:** Governments play a crucial role in establishing clear data privacy and security regulations that provide a framework for responsible data management.

- **Business Practices:** Businesses must prioritize data privacy and security, implementing strong security measures and adhering to ethical guidelines.
- **Research and Development:** Researchers need to focus on developing AI technologies that respect privacy and security, fostering innovation while mitigating risks.
- **Individual Responsibility:** Individuals must be aware of data privacy and security risks, take steps to protect their personal information, and advocate for responsible data practices.

Conclusion: Navigating the Ethical Landscape

Navigating the ethical landscape of AI and data requires a multifaceted approach that combines robust security measures, data privacy regulations, ethical guidelines, technological advancements, and a strong emphasis on education and awareness. By prioritizing responsible data management, we can leverage AI's transformative power while safeguarding individual privacy and ensuring a future where technology empowers humanity.

AI and the Future of Work

AI The specter of job displacement looms large in conversations about AI. It's a natural fear, a haunting echo of the Industrial Revolution, where machines replaced human labor. But the reality of AI's impact on the future of work is far more nuanced and less apocalyptic. It's not about robots stealing jobs, but rather about an evolving job market where certain roles may shift or disappear while new opportunities emerge.

Think of it like a wave: The arrival of AI, while transformative, isn't a sudden tsunami that washes everything away. It's more like a gradual rise in the tide, changing the landscape gradually. Some jobs may be entirely automated, but others will be enhanced and redefined, requiring new skills and adaptations. Imagine a doctor aided by AI to diagnose diseases more accurately, a lawyer leveraging AI to analyze legal documents faster, or an artist collaborating with AI to create unique works of art.

The key to navigating this changing landscape is to embrace the power of upskilling and reskilling. Just as workers during the Industrial Revolution needed to learn new skills to operate machines, we now need to adapt to the demands of an AI-driven world. This means investing in education and training, developing the skills that will be in demand in the future.

But the future isn't solely about technical skills. Soft skills like creativity, critical thinking, and emotional intelligence are becoming increasingly important as AI focuses on tasks that require logic and efficiency. These skills are uniquely human, and they will become even more valuable in a world where AI handles repetitive tasks.

Let's consider some examples:

- **Data Scientists:** As AI becomes more prevalent, the demand for data scientists who can collect, clean, and analyze data to train AI algorithms will only grow.
- **AI Trainers:** These professionals will be responsible for fine-tuning AI models, ensuring that they function

effectively and meet specific performance requirements.

- **AI Ethics Specialists:** As AI technologies become more sophisticated, the need for ethical experts to navigate issues like bias, privacy, and security will be paramount.
- **AI User Experience (UX) Designers:** The user experience of AI applications is crucial for their success. These designers will shape how humans interact with AI systems, ensuring user-friendliness and accessibility.
- **AI-Assisted Writers:** While AI can generate content, it's unlikely to replace the human touch entirely. AI-assisted writers will use AI tools to enhance their creativity and efficiency.
- **AI-Assisted Therapists:** AI can analyze large amounts of data to provide personalized mental health support, but human therapists will remain crucial for empathy and complex emotional support.

In essence, AI is not a threat to our jobs, but rather a catalyst for change. It's an opportunity to redefine work, to embrace new skills, and to create a future where humans and AI collaborate to achieve great things. This shift requires a commitment to learning, adaptation, and a willingness to embrace the potential of AI to enhance our lives and create a better future for all.

The changing job market also presents a significant challenge, one that requires proactive solutions. Governments, educational institutions, and businesses need to work together to equip individuals with the skills they need to succeed in this new world. This means investing in AI education programs, providing opportunities for retraining, and promoting lifelong learning.

Here are some practical steps individuals can take:

- **Stay Informed:** Stay informed about the latest advancements in AI and their potential impact on your field.
- **Learn New Skills:** Invest in online courses, bootcamps, or traditional education to acquire new skills related to AI.
- **Develop Soft Skills:** Focus on developing soft skills like creativity, critical thinking, communication, and emotional intelligence, which are uniquely human and will be in high demand.
- **Embrace AI:** Don't be afraid to use AI tools to enhance your work. Explore how AI can help you be more efficient and creative.
- **Network and Collaborate:** Connect with other professionals in your field and explore opportunities for collaboration.

By embracing this change, we can harness the power of AI to create a more equitable and prosperous future. It's a future where machines and humans work together, amplifying each other's strengths and pushing the boundaries of what's possible.

The Role of Humans in a World of AI

In a world where AI is rapidly advancing, it's crucial to consider the role of humans in this transformative landscape. We're not simply passive observers; we're active participants shaping the future of AI. This chapter explores the potential for humans and AI to collaborate, amplifying each other's strengths and forging a brighter tomorrow.

Imagine a world where AI doesn't replace us, but rather extends our capabilities. Think of a doctor using AI to analyze medical images and identify subtle abnormalities, leading to earlier diagnoses and more effective treatment. Or a scientist leveraging AI to sift through vast amounts of data, accelerating scientific breakthroughs that benefit humanity.

This isn't science fiction; it's the reality we're already experiencing. AI is becoming increasingly sophisticated, capable of performing tasks that were once thought to be exclusive to humans. From drafting emails to composing music, AI is demonstrating its versatility across numerous domains.

But the true power of AI lies not in its ability to replace humans, but in its potential to augment us. By working together, humans and AI can accomplish feats that neither could achieve alone. This collaboration isn't about ceding control; it's about harnessing the unique strengths of each.

Humans possess creativity, empathy, and critical thinking skills – qualities that AI still struggles to emulate. AI, on the other hand, excels at processing vast amounts of data, identifying patterns, and executing tasks with precision and speed. This complementary relationship presents a tremendous opportunity for mutual benefit.

Think of AI as a powerful tool, one that can be used for good or for ill. Its potential is limitless, but so is its potential for harm. This is where the ethical considerations come into play. We must ensure that AI development and deployment prioritize human values – fairness, transparency, and accountability.

The future of AI isn't predetermined; it's being shaped by our choices today. By embracing a collaborative approach, we can guide AI toward a future that empowers humanity, fostering innovation, and addressing the world's most pressing challenges.

One key aspect of this collaboration involves the development of AI systems that are transparent and explainable. Imagine a world where AI-powered decisions are not black boxes, but rather provide clear explanations for their reasoning. This transparency is essential for building trust and ensuring that AI remains accountable to human oversight.

Furthermore, as AI becomes more integrated into our lives, we need to ensure that it aligns with human values and ethical principles. This requires ongoing dialogue and collaboration among experts, policymakers, and the public. We need to address concerns about bias, privacy, and the potential for AI to exacerbate existing societal inequalities.

The future of human-AI collaboration is full of possibilities. Imagine a world where AI assists with complex tasks, allowing us to focus on higher-level thinking and creativity. This collaboration could lead to breakthroughs in medicine, education, and countless other fields.

For example, AI could assist teachers in creating personalized learning plans for students, tailoring educational experiences to their unique needs and learning styles. This would revolutionize education, enabling students to reach their full potential.

Similarly, AI could help scientists analyze massive datasets, leading to new discoveries in fields like medicine, climate science, and astrophysics. By automating tedious tasks, AI would free up scientists to focus on more creative and strategic thinking.

The potential for human-AI collaboration is immense, spanning numerous fields and promising a future where technology augments our capabilities and enhances our lives. But this future requires careful planning, ethical considerations, and ongoing dialogue to ensure that AI development remains aligned with human values and serves the common good.

As we navigate this uncharted territory, it's crucial to embrace the challenges and opportunities of human-AI collaboration. By fostering a partnership where humans and AI work together, we can unlock a future brimming with innovation, prosperity, and a shared sense of purpose.

The future of AI is not predetermined; it's a blank canvas awaiting our collective brushstrokes. Let's ensure that these brushstrokes paint a future where AI empowers humanity, fostering a brighter and more sustainable world for all.

THE FUTURE OF AI ETHICS

As AI becomes increasingly integrated into our lives, the need for ethical guidelines and regulations becomes paramount. The potential benefits of AI are undeniable, but without responsible development and deployment, it could exacerbate existing societal inequalities and create new ethical dilemmas. This is why building a responsible and equitable AI society is a critical endeavor that demands our collective attention and action.

The development and deployment of AI must be guided by a set of core ethical principles that prioritize fairness, accountability, transparency, and inclusivity. This means ensuring that AI systems are designed and used in a way that promotes justice, minimizes harm, and respects human dignity.

One of the most pressing ethical concerns surrounding AI is the potential for bias. AI systems are trained on data, and if this data reflects existing societal biases, the AI system can perpetuate and amplify those biases. For example, an AI system used for loan applications might discriminate against certain demographic groups based on historical data that reflects discriminatory lending practices. It's crucial to address this issue by developing techniques to identify and mitigate bias in training data and algorithms. This might involve techniques like data augmentation, bias detection algorithms, and fairness-aware machine learning.

Furthermore, AI's impact on privacy and security is a significant ethical concern. AI systems often collect and process vast amounts of personal data, raising concerns about data breaches, misuse, and surveillance. We need robust data privacy laws and regulations that ensure individuals have control over their personal data and that AI systems are used in a responsible and transparent manner. This includes implementing strong encryption methods, anonymizing data, and adopting privacy-enhancing technologies.

The future of work is another area where ethical considerations are crucial. AI is automating tasks across various industries, leading to concerns about job displacement and economic inequality. It's essential to invest in education and training programs that prepare individuals for the evolving job market, providing opportunities for reskilling and upskilling. Additionally, we need to consider policies that support a fair and equitable transition to a future where AI plays a significant role in the workforce. This might involve promoting universal basic income, strengthening social safety nets, and providing support for displaced workers.

The role of humans in a world with AI is also critical. AI systems are not intended to replace human judgment and decision-making; they are intended to complement and enhance human capabilities. We need to foster an understanding of AI's capabilities and limitations, promoting collaboration between humans and AI to achieve common goals. This means developing AI systems that are explainable, transparent, and designed to work alongside humans, not replace them.

Building a responsible and equitable AI society requires a multi-faceted approach. Governments, industry leaders, researchers, and individuals must work together to establish ethical guidelines, develop regulations, and promote responsible AI practices. This includes:

- **Developing and implementing ethical guidelines for AI development and deployment:** These guidelines should be based on a set of core principles that prioritize fairness, accountability, transparency, and inclusivity.
- **Establishing regulatory frameworks that address ethical concerns:** This includes laws and regulations that cover data privacy, algorithmic bias, and AI's impact on employment.
- **Investing in research and development of ethical AI technologies:** This includes developing techniques to mitigate bias, ensure transparency, and enhance explainability in AI systems.
- **Promoting public education and awareness about AI and its ethical implications:** This will help individuals make informed decisions about AI and advocate for responsible AI practices.

By actively engaging in these efforts, we can shape a future where AI is a force for good, promoting progress, equity, and a more just and sustainable world. This requires a collective commitment to building a responsible and equitable AI society, one where technology serves humanity, not the other way around.

The future of AI is not predetermined. It's a path that we, as a society, must actively shape. By prioritizing ethical considerations and actively working towards building a responsible and equitable AI society, we can ensure that AI's potential is harnessed for the benefit of all. This requires a collective effort, one that transcends borders, industries, and individual interests. It's a journey that we must embark on together, guided by a shared vision of a future where technology empowers humanity and creates a more just and equitable world for all.

CHAPTER 6

TOOLS AND RESOURCES

AI TOOLS AND PLATFORMS

The world of AI is no longer confined to the realm of science fiction; it's rapidly weaving itself into the fabric of our daily lives. From the personalized recommendations we see on our favorite streaming platforms to the virtual assistants that answer our queries with ease, AI is shaping the way we live, work, and interact with the world around us. But understanding how these technologies work, and how to leverage them for good, requires navigating a complex landscape of tools, platforms, and resources.

This is where "The N.E.R.D.Y. Way" comes in. Chapter 6 of this guide serves as your roadmap, a comprehensive exploration of the AI tools and platforms available to both budding enthusiasts and seasoned professionals. It's like having a personal guide leading you through the vibrant and ever-expanding world of AI development and deployment.

Think of it as your personalized "AI toolbox," packed with the essential instruments to build, shape, and utilize AI solutions. We'll delve into the heart of popular platforms and tools, unveiling their strengths, applications, and potential limitations. You'll learn how to use these tools effectively, how to choose the right one for your needs, and how to stay ahead of the curve as the landscape continues to evolve.

But this chapter is more than just a technical guide. It's about empowering you to embrace the creative potential of AI. By exploring the tools and platforms available, you'll gain the confidence to experiment, innovate, and even contribute to shaping the future of this transformative technology.

Let's start by diving into the diverse ecosystem of AI platforms. These are the foundations upon which you build your AI solutions, the frameworks that provide the necessary tools and infrastructure for development and deployment. They're like the scaffolding around a building, providing the structure and support for your project.

Cloud-Based AI Platforms: Powering AI at Scale

Imagine having access to a vast library of AI tools and services, ready to be deployed with a few clicks. Cloud-based AI platforms make this dream a reality. These platforms provide the computing power, storage, and infrastructure needed for even the most complex AI tasks.

1. **Google Cloud AI Platform:** This platform is a powerhouse, offering a comprehensive suite of tools and services for building, deploying, and managing AI models. From Google's cutting-edge machine learning

algorithms to its advanced data analytics tools, you have the resources to tackle any AI challenge.

2. **Amazon SageMaker:** Amazon's AI platform is designed for both beginners and experts. It provides pre-trained models, ready-to-use algorithms, and customizable infrastructure, making it easy to get started with AI development.

3. **Microsoft Azure AI:** Microsoft's platform offers a blend of accessibility and power, with a focus on responsible AI development. It provides tools for data labeling, model training, and responsible AI practices, ensuring you build ethical and impactful AI solutions.

4. **IBM Watson:** Known for its cognitive computing capabilities, IBM Watson offers a range of AI services, including natural language processing, machine learning, and data analysis. This platform is a favorite for organizations looking to integrate AI into their business operations.

5. **Alibaba Cloud AI:** This platform is rapidly gaining traction, offering a range of AI tools and services for a global audience. It provides solutions for image recognition, natural language processing, and other AI applications, supporting a growing community of developers.

Open-Source AI Platforms: A Collaborative Ecosystem

Not all AI development needs to be proprietary. Open-source AI platforms foster a collaborative environment, allowing developers to share code, algorithms, and expertise freely.

1. **TensorFlow:** Developed by Google, TensorFlow is one of the most popular open-source platforms for machine learning. It offers a flexible and scalable framework for building and deploying AI models across various applications.
2. **PyTorch:** Developed by Facebook, PyTorch is another popular open-source platform. It's known for its user-friendly interface and its ability to seamlessly integrate with Python, making it a favorite among researchers and developers.
3. **Keras:** While Keras is a high-level API for building deep learning models, it's often used in conjunction with TensorFlow or Theano. Its intuitive design makes it easy to create complex neural networks, even for those new to deep learning.
4. **Scikit-learn:** This platform is a staple for machine learning in Python. It provides a comprehensive collection of algorithms for classification, regression, clustering, and other machine learning tasks.
5. **Apache MXNet:** This platform offers a high-performance, scalable framework for building and deploying AI models. It's designed for large-scale machine learning projects, supporting distributed training and deployment.

Specialized AI Platforms: Focusing on Specific Applications

The AI landscape is not monolithic. Specialized platforms cater to specific applications, offering tailored tools and services to address industry-specific challenges.

1. **Google Dialogflow:** This platform is specifically designed for building conversational AI applications, such as chatbots and virtual assistants. It offers tools for natural language understanding, intent recognition, and dialogue management.
2. **Amazon Rekognition:** Focusing on computer vision, Amazon Rekognition provides tools for image and video analysis, including object detection, facial recognition, and scene understanding.
3. **Microsoft Azure Cognitive Services:** This suite of services offers a range of AI capabilities, including vision, speech, language, and knowledge APIs. They're designed for seamless integration with other Microsoft products and services.
4. **IBM Maximo Asset Management:** This platform leverages AI to optimize asset management, predict failures, and improve operational efficiency. It's a valuable tool for industries with complex assets, such as manufacturing, utilities, and transportation.
5. **DeepMind's AlphaFold:** While not a platform in the traditional sense, AlphaFold's groundbreaking AI system revolutionized protein structure prediction, offering a glimpse into the potential of AI in scientific discovery.

AI Tools: Unlocking the Power of AI

AI tools are the building blocks of AI applications, providing the specific functions and capabilities needed to process data, train models, and deploy solutions.

1. **Data Labeling Tools:** Data labeling is essential for training supervised machine learning models. These tools streamline the process of annotating data, allowing you to create high-quality datasets for model training.
2. **Model Training Tools:** These tools provide the environment and resources needed to train machine learning models. They offer various algorithms, optimization techniques, and hyperparameter tuning options to maximize model performance.
3. **Model Deployment Tools:** Once your AI model is trained, you need to deploy it for real-world use. Deployment tools provide the infrastructure and mechanisms to integrate your model into applications, APIs, or cloud services.
4. **AI Development Environments:** These environments provide the integrated development environment (IDE) and other tools needed for AI development. They often include features like code editors, debugging tools, and libraries to simplify the development process.
5. **AI Explainability Tools:** As AI models become increasingly complex, it's essential to understand how they arrive at their decisions. Explainability tools help uncover the inner workings of AI models, making them more transparent and accountable.

Beyond the Tools: Developing Your Skills

The tools and platforms are powerful, but they're only as effective as the people using them. Acquiring the necessary AI skills is essential to leverage these resources effectively and to contribute to the future of AI.

1. **Online Courses and Bootcamps:** Numerous online platforms, such as Coursera, Udacity, and edX, offer comprehensive courses on AI, machine learning, deep learning, and other related topics. Bootcamps provide immersive, hands-on training programs to accelerate your AI skills development.

2. **AI Books and Articles:** The world of AI literature is vast, offering a wealth of knowledge for every level of expertise. From introductory guides to advanced textbooks, you can find resources to delve deeper into specific AI concepts and techniques.

3. **AI Communities and Forums:** Connecting with other AI enthusiasts and professionals is essential for learning and staying up-to-date. Online communities and forums provide a platform for asking questions, sharing insights, and collaborating on AI projects.

4. **AI Conferences and Events:** Attending AI conferences and events is a great way to network with experts, learn about the latest advancements, and gain insights into emerging trends.

5. **Hands-on Projects:** The best way to learn AI is by doing. Start with small projects to build your skills, experiment with different tools and platforms, and develop your understanding of AI concepts in a practical setting.

The Future of AI Tools and Platforms

The AI landscape is in constant flux, with new tools, platforms, and resources emerging all the time. Staying informed about the latest advancements is essential to remain competitive and to harness the full potential of AI.

1. **AI-powered Development Tools:** AI is even being used to develop AI tools, leading to more intuitive, automated, and efficient development workflows.
2. **Edge AI Platforms:** As AI applications become more ubiquitous, there's a growing need for AI to operate on edge devices, such as smartphones and IoT sensors. Edge AI platforms are emerging to address this need, enabling AI to function in resource-constrained environments.
3. **AI Ethics and Governance Tools:** The responsible development and deployment of AI are crucial. Tools are emerging to help ensure fairness, transparency, and accountability in AI systems.
4. **AI for Scientific Discovery:** AI is revolutionizing scientific research, leading to breakthroughs in areas such as drug discovery, materials science, and climate modeling. New tools and platforms are emerging to support AI-driven research.
5. **AI Democratization:** The goal of AI democratization is to make AI accessible to everyone, regardless of technical expertise. New tools and platforms are being developed to lower the barrier to entry for AI development and deployment.

The journey into the world of AI can feel overwhelming at times. But by embracing the "N.E.R.D.Y. Way" – through knowledge, education, resources, and discovery – you'll be well-equipped to navigate this exciting and transformative landscape. Remember, AI is not just about technology; it's about unlocking human potential, pushing the boundaries of what's possible, and shaping a future where technology empowers humanity.

AI AND LIBRARIES AND FRAMEWORKS

Imagine a world where developers, armed with the right tools, can weave complex AI algorithms with ease. This is the world of AI libraries and frameworks, powerful tools that empower developers to build sophisticated AI applications without needing to start from scratch.

Think of these libraries and frameworks as pre-built blocks, each designed to tackle a specific challenge in AI development. They provide a foundation of pre-written code, algorithms, and functionalities, allowing developers to focus on solving problems rather than reinventing the wheel.

This chapter delves into the world of AI libraries and frameworks, exploring how they've revolutionized AI development and empowering developers to create groundbreaking solutions. We'll unravel the intricate workings of these tools, highlighting their diverse capabilities and explaining how they simplify the development process, accelerate innovation, and unleash the full potential of AI.

The Foundation of AI Development

AI libraries and frameworks are the cornerstone of modern AI development. They provide developers with a vast collection of pre-built tools and components, simplifying the process of building complex AI systems. These tools can be broadly categorized into two groups:

- **Libraries:** Collections of pre-written code and functions that developers can directly integrate into their projects. They offer a range of functionalities, from basic data manipulation and mathematical operations to advanced machine learning algorithms and model training tools.
- **Frameworks:** Provide a structured environment for building and deploying AI applications. They offer a high-level abstraction, allowing developers to focus on the overall architecture and design of their AI systems while handling low-level implementation details in the background.

Popular AI Libraries and Frameworks

The AI landscape is teeming with libraries and frameworks, each with its strengths and unique applications. Let's explore some of the most prominent players:

- **TensorFlow:** Developed by Google, TensorFlow is a versatile and popular library for building and deploying machine learning models. Its flexible architecture allows developers to create models for various tasks, including image recognition, natural language processing, and time series analysis. TensorFlow provides a rich ecosystem of pre-trained models and tools, accelerating the development process.
- **PyTorch:** Another popular library, PyTorch, offers a dynamic computational graph that provides flexibility

and ease of use. It's particularly well-suited for research and experimentation, allowing developers to iterate quickly and test different models. PyTorch also boasts a vibrant community and extensive documentation, making it a popular choice for researchers and developers.

- **Keras:** While often classified as a library, Keras is more accurately described as a high-level API that simplifies the use of other libraries like TensorFlow and Theano. It provides a user-friendly interface, enabling developers to build and train deep learning models with minimal code.

- **Scikit-learn:** A comprehensive library focused on machine learning tasks, Scikit-learn provides algorithms for classification, regression, clustering, and dimensionality reduction. It's ideal for beginners who want to explore the world of machine learning or for experienced developers who need a robust library for building traditional machine learning models.

- **OpenCV:** Dedicated to computer vision applications, OpenCV offers a wide range of tools for image and video processing, object detection, and facial recognition. It's widely used in industries like robotics, surveillance, and autonomous driving.

- **NLTK:** A powerful library for natural language processing, NLTK provides tools for tasks like text classification, sentiment analysis, and machine translation. It's widely used in fields like linguistics, computer science, and artificial intelligence.

- **SpaCy:** Another natural language processing library, SpaCy focuses on efficiency and speed. It provides tools for tokenization, part-of-speech tagging, named entity recognition, and dependency parsing. It's often used for text analysis, information extraction, and machine translation.

The Benefits of AI Libraries and Frameworks

The adoption of AI libraries and frameworks has ushered in a new era of AI development, providing developers with numerous benefits:

- **Faster Development:** Libraries and frameworks eliminate the need to write code from scratch, allowing developers to focus on solving problems rather than building the basic infrastructure. This significantly reduces development time, accelerating innovation.
- **Simplified Implementation:** Libraries and frameworks handle complex tasks behind the scenes, such as memory management, resource allocation, and optimization. This frees developers from the burden of low-level details, allowing them to concentrate on the logic and design of their AI systems.
- **Enhanced Productivity:** By providing a structured environment and pre-built components, libraries and frameworks streamline the development process, enabling developers to build sophisticated AI applications more efficiently.
- **Access to Pre-trained Models:** Libraries and frameworks often offer pre-trained models, allowing developers to leverage the knowledge gained from vast datasets. This eliminates the need for extensive training, saving time and resources.

- **Collaboration and Community:** The wide adoption of libraries and frameworks has fostered a vibrant community of developers. This collaborative environment facilitates knowledge sharing, problem-solving, and the development of new tools and resources.

Navigating the AI Library and Framework Landscape

The sheer variety of AI libraries and frameworks can be overwhelming for beginners. Here are some tips to navigate this diverse landscape:

- **Define your project goals:** Before choosing a library or framework, clearly define the specific problem you're trying to solve and the desired outcomes.
- **Research your options:** Explore different libraries and frameworks, comparing their features, functionalities, and strengths. Consider factors like performance, ease of use, community support, and documentation.
- **Start with a simple example:** Most libraries and frameworks provide tutorials and examples to help you get started quickly. Start with a basic example to gain a foundational understanding of the tool.
- **Don't be afraid to experiment:** Explore different libraries and frameworks to find the one that best suits your needs and workflow.
- **Join the community:** Connect with other developers using the same library or framework. Participate in online forums, attend conferences, and contribute to

open-source projects to enhance your skills and knowledge.

The Future of AI Libraries and Frameworks

As AI continues to evolve at an accelerated pace, we can expect even more powerful and sophisticated libraries and frameworks to emerge. These tools will further simplify the development process, enabling developers to create increasingly advanced and intelligent applications.

The future of AI libraries and frameworks holds immense promise. They will not only accelerate the development of AI applications but also democratize access to AI, empowering a broader range of developers to contribute to the advancement of this transformative technology. By leveraging these powerful tools, developers can unlock the full potential of AI, creating solutions that address real-world challenges and shape a brighter future.

AI EDUCATION AND TRAINING

The world of artificial intelligence is rapidly evolving, offering a vast array of opportunities for those who wish to dive in and explore its possibilities. But for many, the path to entering this exciting field can feel daunting. Where does one begin? How do you acquire the necessary skills to navigate this complex world? Fear not, dear reader! This chapter will serve as your guide, leading you through the landscape of AI education and training resources, unveiling a world brimming with knowledge and empowering you to take your first steps into the exciting world of AI.

Imagine stepping into a bustling marketplace brimming with vendors offering an array of tools, technologies, and learning materials, each promising to unlock the secrets of AI. It's an exciting landscape, but it can also be overwhelming. This chapter is your personal shopper, guiding you through the aisles, highlighting the best resources, and helping you identify the tools and training options that best suit your needs and ambitions. We'll embark on a journey to uncover the hidden gems of the AI learning world, from renowned online platforms and immersive bootcamps to vibrant communities and forums where you can connect with fellow enthusiasts and experts.

First, let's delve into the world of online courses, a popular gateway to AI education. These courses offer flexible learning paths, allowing you to acquire knowledge at your own pace and convenience. Online platforms like Coursera, edX, Udacity, and Udemy are home to a wealth of AI courses, catering to different learning styles and levels of experience. Whether you're a complete beginner or a seasoned professional seeking to expand your AI skills, these platforms have something for everyone.

Coursera

Coursera, a leading online learning platform, boasts a diverse selection of AI courses offered by top universities and institutions worldwide. You'll find everything from introductory courses on the fundamentals of AI to specialized programs focusing on specific AI applications like machine learning, deep learning, natural language processing, and computer vision.

One of the most popular Coursera AI courses is "Machine Learning" by Stanford University. This course covers the essential principles of machine learning, including supervised learning, unsupervised learning, and reinforcement learning, and provides a comprehensive overview of algorithms and techniques used in modern AI applications.

Another popular Coursera offering is "Deep Learning Specialization" by deeplearning.ai, a renowned AI research and education company. This specialization program provides a deep dive into the world of deep learning, covering topics like neural networks, convolutional neural networks, recurrent neural networks, and generative adversarial networks (GANs).

edX

edX, another prominent online learning platform, collaborates with leading universities and research institutions to offer a rich array of AI courses. You'll find courses on topics like machine learning, artificial intelligence, computer vision, and robotics, with various options catering to different levels of expertise.

One notable edX AI course is "Introduction to Artificial Intelligence" offered by the University of California, Berkeley. This course provides a broad introduction to AI, covering fundamental concepts, history, and applications across various industries.

Another noteworthy edX offering is "Machine Learning for Data Science and Analytics" by the University of Washington. This course delves into the use of machine learning for data analysis and decision-making, equipping students with practical skills in data mining, prediction, and optimization.

Udacity

Udacity is a platform specializing in technical skills development, offering a curated selection of AI nanodegree programs. These programs provide comprehensive training in specific AI fields, offering hands-on experience and project-based learning to solidify your knowledge.

Udacity's "Machine Learning Engineer Nanodegree" program covers the essential aspects of machine learning, providing practical skills in developing and deploying machine learning models.

Their "Deep Learning Nanodegree" program focuses on the fundamentals of deep learning, covering neural networks, convolutional neural networks, recurrent neural networks, and other key concepts.

Udemy

Udemy, a vast platform with a diverse selection of online courses, offers a wide range of AI courses catering to different needs and interests. You'll find both introductory courses and more specialized programs, covering topics like machine learning, deep learning, natural language processing, and computer vision.

Udemy's "Complete Machine Learning & Data Science Bootcamp 2023" is a comprehensive course covering a broad range of data science and machine learning topics.

Their "Deep Learning A-Z™: Hands-On Artificial Neural Networks" course delves into the world of deep learning, providing practical insights and hands-on experience with neural networks.

While online courses offer flexibility and accessibility, you may be seeking a more immersive and interactive learning experience. In that case, AI bootcamps might be the perfect fit for you. Bootcamps provide intensive, hands-on training, often delivered in a condensed format over several weeks or months. They typically involve a mix of lectures, hands-on projects, and real-world application exercises, allowing you to dive deep into the practical aspects of AI.

AI Bootcamps

The AI bootcamp landscape is expanding rapidly, with numerous options catering to different career paths and levels of experience. These bootcamps are designed to equip individuals with the skills and knowledge needed to excel in the competitive world of AI, whether you're aiming to transition into an AI-related career or enhance your existing skills.

- **General Assembly**: General Assembly is a well-known provider of bootcamps across various disciplines, including data science and AI. Their AI bootcamps cover topics like machine learning, deep learning, and natural language processing, providing a comprehensive training experience with a focus on practical application.
- **DataCamp**: DataCamp, known for its data science courses, also offers specialized bootcamps in AI and machine learning. Their bootcamps provide an immersive learning experience, covering topics like supervised learning, unsupervised learning, and reinforcement learning, with a focus on practical applications and projects.
- **Le Wagon**: Le Wagon is a global bootcamp provider offering a data science program that includes a significant focus on AI and machine learning. Their program emphasizes hands-on learning, projects, and real-world applications, preparing graduates for successful careers in data science and AI.

- **Springboard**: Springboard offers a career-oriented bootcamp in machine learning, emphasizing practical skills and portfolio development. Their program combines live instruction, personalized mentorship, and project-based learning, preparing graduates for success in the competitive world of AI.

Other Resources

Beyond online courses and bootcamps, there are numerous other resources available to bolster your AI education and training.

- **Books**: The world of AI literature is vast, offering a wide range of books catering to different levels of expertise and interests. From introductory guides for beginners to more advanced texts covering specific AI fields, there's a book for every learner. Popular AI books include "Deep Learning" by Ian Goodfellow, Yoshua Bengio, and Aaron Courville, "Hands-On Machine Learning with Scikit-Learn, Keras & TensorFlow" by Aurélien Géron, "Artificial Intelligence: A Modern Approach" by Stuart Russell and Peter Norvig, and "The Master Algorithm" by Pedro Domingos.

- **Online Tutorials and Resources**: The internet is a treasure trove of AI resources, from tutorials and blog posts to open-source libraries and frameworks. Websites like Google's TensorFlow Tutorials, the PyTorch Tutorials, the Keras Documentation, and the Scikit-learn User Guide provide comprehensive resources for learning and applying AI techniques.

- **YouTube Channels**: YouTube is a fantastic platform for exploring AI concepts and tutorials. Channels like "3Blue1Brown," "Two Minute Papers," "Siraj Raval," "sentdex," and "Lex Fridman" provide engaging videos explaining AI concepts, showcasing new research, and conducting interviews with leading AI experts.
- **Podcasts**: Podcasts are a convenient way to stay up-to-date on the latest AI trends, research, and applications. Popular AI podcasts include "The AI Podcast," "Talking Machines," "Data Skeptic," and "Artificial Intelligence in Industry."
- **Conferences and Workshops**: Attending AI conferences and workshops provides an opportunity to network with industry professionals, learn about the latest advancements, and gain insights into emerging trends. Conferences like the NeurIPS (Neural Information Processing Systems), ICML (International Conference on Machine Learning), and the AAAI (Association for the Advancement of Artificial Intelligence) are prominent events that draw together top researchers, developers, and practitioners.

Community and Networks

One of the most rewarding aspects of learning about AI is the opportunity to connect with a vibrant community of enthusiasts and professionals. Engaging with this community can help you learn, share insights, and stay up-to-date on the latest advancements.

- **Online Forums**: Online forums like Reddit's r/MachineLearning, r/ArtificialIntelligence, and r/DeepLearning provide a platform for engaging in discussions, seeking advice, and sharing experiences with other AI enthusiasts.

- **Slack Groups**: Numerous Slack groups are dedicated to AI, offering channels for discussions, sharing resources, and networking with fellow professionals.
- **Meetups**: AI meetups are held in cities worldwide, providing a physical space to connect with other enthusiasts, attend talks, and engage in hands-on workshops.

Staying Ahead of the Curve

The world of AI is constantly evolving, with new tools, platforms, and resources emerging regularly. To stay ahead of the curve, it's crucial to remain curious, embrace lifelong learning, and continuously explore new opportunities for growth.

- **Newsletters and Blogs**: AI-focused newsletters and blogs provide a convenient way to stay informed about the latest trends, research, and advancements. Popular AI newsletters and blogs include "The Batch," "Towards Data Science," "Machine Learning Mastery," "Analytics Vidhya," and "AI Weekly."
- **AI Conferences**: Attending AI conferences is an excellent way to stay informed about cutting-edge research, emerging trends, and practical applications.
- **Online Communities**: Engaging with online communities and forums allows you to connect with other enthusiasts, share insights, and learn about the latest developments.

As you embark on your AI journey, remember that it's not a sprint, but a marathon. Embrace the learning process, celebrate your progress, and don't be afraid to ask for help along the way. The AI world is brimming with opportunities, waiting for you to explore. So, dive in, explore, and let your curiosity guide you! With the right resources and a thirst for knowledge, you too can unlock the power of AI and shape a future where technology empowers humanity.

AI Community and Networks

The AI community is a vibrant and ever-growing ecosystem of individuals passionate about artificial intelligence. It's a place where knowledge is shared, ideas are exchanged, and collaboration thrives. For anyone interested in exploring the world of AI, joining this community is an invaluable step.

Imagine a bustling online marketplace where experts, enthusiasts, and learners come together to share their knowledge, insights, and experiences. This is what online AI communities offer – a platform to connect, learn, and grow. These communities are a treasure trove of information, offering access to the latest research, discussions on emerging trends, and practical tips and tricks from seasoned professionals.

Here's a glimpse into the diverse landscape of online AI communities:

- **Forums:** Forums like Reddit's r/artificialintelligence, r/MachineLearning, and r/deeplearning are bustling hubs for discussions on various AI topics. From technical discussions on specific algorithms to philosophical debates on AI ethics, these forums offer a platform for users to ask questions, share insights, and engage in lively debates.

- **Online Communities:** Platforms like Kaggle, a data science and machine learning competition platform, provide a space for users to collaborate on projects, share their work, and learn from each other. You can find insightful tutorials, data sets, and projects that cater to various skill levels.
- **Meetup Groups:** Meetup groups offer a chance to connect with fellow AI enthusiasts in your local area. These groups organize events like workshops, hackathons, and networking sessions, providing a face-to-face opportunity to learn and collaborate.
- **Online Courses and Bootcamps:** Platforms like Coursera, edX, and Udacity offer comprehensive courses and bootcamps on AI, machine learning, and deep learning. These platforms often provide forums and communities where students can interact with instructors, peers, and industry experts.
- **Professional Networks:** LinkedIn and Twitter are excellent platforms for connecting with AI professionals and staying updated on industry news. You can follow thought leaders, participate in discussions, and network with professionals in your field.

Beyond the Online Realm

The AI community extends beyond the virtual world. Conferences, workshops, and hackathons provide a platform for in-person networking and knowledge sharing. Attending these events gives you the opportunity to meet experts, learn about cutting-edge research, and participate in hands-on projects.

- **Conferences:** Conferences like NeurIPS, ICML, and CVPR are renowned gatherings for researchers, developers, and industry professionals to share their latest findings and explore the future of AI.
- **Workshops:** Workshops offer a more focused learning experience, providing hands-on training on specific AI tools, techniques, and applications. These workshops are often led by industry experts and provide an opportunity to gain practical skills.
- **Hackathons:** Hackathons are intense events where participants come together to solve real-world problems using AI. These events foster creativity, collaboration, and rapid innovation, allowing you to test your skills and develop new solutions.

Benefits of Joining the AI Community

- **Enhanced Learning:** Engaging with the AI community exposes you to a vast pool of knowledge, providing access to diverse perspectives, insights, and resources.
- **Networking Opportunities:** Connecting with fellow AI enthusiasts opens doors to collaborations, mentorship, and career opportunities.
- **Staying Ahead of the Curve:** Participating in discussions and following industry trends helps you stay informed about the latest advancements and emerging technologies in the field.

- **Practical Experience:** Participating in hackathons and collaborative projects provides valuable hands-on experience, allowing you to apply your knowledge and develop your skills.
- **Inspiration and Motivation:** Surrounding yourself with like-minded individuals can be incredibly inspiring and motivating, fostering your passion for AI and encouraging you to pursue your goals.

How to Get Involved

- **Choose your preferred platform:** Identify online communities, forums, or social media platforms that align with your interests and skill level.
- **Engage in discussions:** Participate in forums, ask questions, share your insights, and engage in lively debates with fellow enthusiasts.
- **Contribute to projects:** Collaborate on open-source projects or participate in hackathons to gain practical experience and contribute to the development of AI applications.
- **Attend events:** Attend conferences, workshops, and meetups to connect with industry experts and learn from their experience.
- **Follow industry leaders:** Stay updated on the latest advancements and trends by following thought leaders and industry influencers.

The AI community is a dynamic and welcoming environment for individuals of all backgrounds and skill levels. By joining this community, you can accelerate your learning, expand your network, and become part of a movement shaping the future of technology. So, take the leap, engage, and contribute to the vibrant world of AI!

The Future of AI Resources

The landscape of AI resources is constantly evolving, with new tools, platforms, and communities emerging at a rapid pace. This dynamic environment presents both opportunities and challenges for those who want to stay ahead of the curve in the world of AI. To navigate this exciting landscape, it's essential to embrace a mindset of continuous learning and exploration.

Staying informed about the latest AI resources requires a multi-pronged approach. We can leverage various tools and platforms to stay connected to the latest developments, engage with the AI community, and expand our knowledge through educational resources.

Staying Connected with the Latest Advancements

The world of AI is constantly evolving, with new breakthroughs, innovations, and research emerging regularly. To keep up with this fast-paced field, it's crucial to access reliable sources of information.

- **AI News and Blogs:** Stay abreast of the latest AI trends, research, and industry updates by subscribing to leading AI news outlets and blogs. These publications provide insightful analyses, feature articles, and summaries of groundbreaking research.
- **AI Research Papers and Preprints:** Access the latest research papers and preprints from renowned academic institutions and research organizations. Online

platforms like arXiv.org serve as repositories for preprints, allowing researchers to share their findings before formal publication.

- **AI Conferences and Workshops:** Attend industry conferences, workshops, and seminars focused on AI. These events bring together leading experts, researchers, and practitioners, offering valuable insights into the latest advancements and emerging trends.

Exploring AI Tools and Platforms

AI tools and platforms are essential for developers, researchers, and businesses looking to leverage the power of AI. These tools provide a range of capabilities, from data processing and analysis to model training and deployment.

- **Cloud AI Platforms:** Cloud providers such as Google Cloud Platform, Amazon Web Services, and Microsoft Azure offer comprehensive AI platforms that include pre-trained models, APIs, and tools for building and deploying AI applications. These platforms simplify the process of developing and deploying AI solutions, making them accessible to a wider range of users.
- **Open-Source AI Libraries and Frameworks:** The open-source community plays a vital role in advancing the field of AI. Numerous open-source libraries and frameworks, such as TensorFlow, PyTorch, and scikit-learn, provide tools and resources for building AI applications. These libraries offer a wide range of functionalities, including data processing, model training, and model evaluation.

- **AI Development Tools and IDEs:** Specialized AI development tools and integrated development environments (IDEs) provide developers with a streamlined and efficient workflow for building AI applications. These tools offer features such as debugging, code completion, and visualization, simplifying the development process.

Expanding Your AI Skills and Knowledge

Continuous learning is essential for staying ahead of the curve in the rapidly evolving field of AI. Fortunately, numerous resources are available to help individuals enhance their AI skills and knowledge.

- **Online AI Courses and Bootcamps:** Online learning platforms like Coursera, Udacity, and edX offer a wide range of AI courses and bootcamps, catering to different skill levels and interests. These courses provide structured learning paths, covering theoretical concepts and practical skills.
- **AI Books and Tutorials:** Explore a diverse range of books and tutorials dedicated to various aspects of AI, from introductory concepts to advanced techniques. These resources provide in-depth explanations, practical examples, and code snippets to help readers grasp the fundamentals and apply their knowledge.
- **AI Communities and Forums:** Engage with the vibrant AI community by joining online forums, discussion groups, and social media communities. These platforms provide opportunities to ask

questions, share knowledge, and learn from other AI enthusiasts and professionals.

Building a Network of AI Professionals

Networking is essential for staying connected to the AI ecosystem and expanding your professional horizons.

- **AI Meetup Groups:** Connect with other AI professionals and enthusiasts in your local area by attending AI meetups and workshops. These events offer opportunities for collaboration, knowledge sharing, and networking.
- **AI LinkedIn Groups:** Join LinkedIn groups focused on AI to connect with professionals in your field. These groups provide access to industry updates, job postings, and discussions on relevant topics.

Embracing a Growth Mindset:

Staying ahead of the curve in the ever-evolving world of AI requires a growth mindset, a commitment to continuous learning, and a willingness to adapt to new technologies and trends. Embrace this journey of discovery, and you'll be well-positioned to navigate the exciting future of AI.

C H A P T E R 7

T H E N.E.R.D.Y. W A Y: E M B R A C I N G T H E F U T U R E

T H E P O W E R O F A I F O R G O O D

The Imagine a world where AI is not just a tool, but a powerful ally in addressing some of the most pressing challenges facing humanity. This isn't a futuristic fantasy; it's a reality rapidly unfolding before our eyes. The potential of AI for good is immense, and it's time to harness its power to tackle global issues like climate change, poverty, and disease.

Let's start with climate change. AI can be a game-changer in understanding and mitigating its devastating effects. With its ability to analyze massive datasets, AI can identify patterns in climate data, predict future trends, and develop innovative solutions for reducing greenhouse gas emissions. Imagine AI-powered systems optimizing energy consumption in buildings, optimizing transportation routes to minimize fuel usage, and even predicting extreme weather events to better prepare for their impact.

Beyond prediction, AI can accelerate the development of renewable energy sources. By analyzing vast amounts of data from research labs and field experiments, AI can help scientists design more efficient solar panels, wind turbines, and other clean energy technologies. It can even optimize the placement of these technologies, maximizing their effectiveness and ensuring efficient energy distribution.

But AI's potential goes beyond combating climate change. Its transformative power can also be leveraged to alleviate poverty and inequality. AI can help develop targeted social programs by analyzing demographic data and identifying individuals and communities most in need of assistance. For instance, AI-powered systems can analyze income levels, healthcare access, and education attainment to create personalized intervention programs tailored to specific needs. This can lead to more equitable distribution of resources and opportunities, fostering social mobility and reducing poverty.

In the realm of healthcare, AI holds immense promise for improving patient outcomes and expanding access to quality care. AI-powered diagnostic tools can analyze medical images, such as X-rays and scans, with greater accuracy than human experts, helping doctors detect diseases at earlier stages. This can lead to faster and more effective treatment, improving survival rates and overall patient well-being.

AI can also revolutionize drug discovery and development. By analyzing vast databases of molecular structures and biological pathways, AI can identify potential drug candidates and predict their effectiveness. This can accelerate the process of developing new medications, bringing life-saving treatments to patients faster. Additionally, AI can personalize medicine by analyzing an individual's genetic makeup and medical history to create personalized treatment plans.

AI's power extends to providing access to healthcare in remote and underserved communities. Telemedicine platforms powered by AI can enable doctors to diagnose and treat patients remotely, bridging the gap in healthcare access and ensuring quality care for everyone. This is especially crucial in regions with limited access to medical professionals, allowing people in remote areas to receive timely and accurate medical care.

The potential of AI for good is vast, extending beyond these examples. It can help address global challenges like hunger, education, and water scarcity. For instance, AI can optimize agricultural practices by analyzing soil conditions, weather patterns, and crop health data, leading to increased food production and reduced waste.

AI can personalize education, tailoring learning materials and teaching methods to individual student needs. It can even develop intelligent tutoring systems that provide personalized support, helping students achieve their full potential. And, AI can analyze water resource data to predict potential shortages and develop strategies for managing water resources more effectively, ensuring access to clean water for all.

As we embrace the future of AI, it's crucial to recognize its transformative potential for good. By harnessing its power responsibly and ethically, we can unlock its ability to address global challenges, create a more sustainable and equitable world, and build a future where technology empowers humanity. This isn't just a dream; it's a responsibility we must embrace, a future we must actively shape. Let us leverage the power of AI for good and create a world where technology serves as a force for positive change, driving progress for generations to come.

THE HUMAN-AI PARTNERSHIP

The human-AI partnership is not just a theoretical concept; it's a tangible reality shaping the future across various fields. It's about leveraging AI's unique strengths – its ability to process vast amounts of data, identify patterns, and make predictions – to complement and enhance human capabilities. This collaboration is not about replacing humans; it's about empowering them to achieve more.

Imagine a world where AI assists doctors in diagnosing diseases more accurately and quickly, leading to better patient outcomes. AI-powered systems can analyze medical images, predict potential health risks, and even personalize treatment plans based on individual patient data. This collaboration empowers doctors to make more informed decisions and dedicate more time to providing personalized care.

AI can also revolutionize industries like finance, where it can analyze market trends, detect fraudulent activities, and manage investments more efficiently. Human financial experts can use AI insights to make data-driven decisions, mitigate risk, and maximize returns. This partnership allows them to focus on complex financial strategies and build long-term relationships with clients.

Beyond specific industries, the human-AI partnership can help us address global challenges. AI can help us model climate change scenarios, develop sustainable energy solutions, and design smart cities that optimize resource usage. In agriculture,

AI can optimize crop yields, reduce water consumption, and improve food security.

But the power of this collaboration goes beyond solving problems; it's about unleashing human creativity and innovation. AI can assist artists in generating new ideas, composing music, and creating visually stunning artwork. It can help writers overcome writer's block and explore different narrative possibilities. This partnership can foster a new era of artistic expression, where AI becomes a tool for creative exploration and exploration.

The human-AI partnership is not without its challenges. We must address concerns about bias in AI algorithms, ensure data privacy and security, and prepare for the potential impact on the job market. However, by embracing collaboration and actively shaping the development and deployment of AI, we can harness its power for good.

The future belongs to those who are willing to embrace the human-AI partnership. It's a future where AI amplifies our intelligence, creativity, and problem-solving abilities, enabling us to achieve things we couldn't imagine before. It's a future where humans and AI work together to build a better world for everyone.

A Call to Action

The possibilities of AI are boundless, reaching across industries and touching every aspect of our lives. But AI's future is not predetermined; it's in our hands to shape it, to ensure it serves humanity's best interests. This is where you come in.

Imagine a world where AI is harnessed to combat climate change, where personalized medicine eradicates diseases, where education is tailored to each student's unique needs, and where self-driving cars create a safer, more efficient transportation system. This is not just a dream; it's a future we can build together.

But building this future requires active participation, a willingness to learn, and a commitment to responsible development. Here's how you can contribute:

- **Become an AI Advocate:** Educate yourself and others about AI. Share your knowledge, dispel myths, and advocate for ethical AI practices. Start conversations, engage in online discussions, and participate in community events.
- **Explore AI Resources:** Dive into the vast world of AI tools, platforms, and resources. Experiment with AI programming, learn about machine learning algorithms, and explore the diverse applications of AI across different fields. There are countless online courses, tutorials, and communities dedicated to AI education. Embrace this opportunity to expand your knowledge and hone your skills.
- **Join the AI Community:** Connect with other AI enthusiasts, researchers, and developers. Collaborate on projects, exchange ideas, and participate in hackathons. Networking is crucial in any field, but it's especially valuable in the rapidly evolving world of AI. By collaborating and sharing knowledge, we can accelerate the development of beneficial AI solutions.
- **Champion Ethical AI:** Be a voice for responsible AI development and deployment. Advocate for ethical guidelines, transparency in AI systems, and data

privacy protection. Participate in discussions about AI's impact on society, raise awareness about potential risks, and contribute to shaping a future where AI is used for good.

Remember, AI is not just about technology; it's about people. It's about how we use technology to solve problems, empower individuals, and create a better future for all. Your voice, your creativity, and your dedication are crucial to building a responsible and equitable AI society.

This isn't about becoming an expert; it's about starting a conversation, asking questions, exploring possibilities, and taking action. The future of AI is not preordained; it's up to each of us to shape it.

So, embrace the "N.E.R.D.Y. Way." Be curious, be informed, be involved. Together, let's create a world where AI empowers humanity, advances progress, and fosters a better future.

The N.E.R.D.Y. Way

The N.E.R.D.Y. Way, a potent acronym that stands for Knowledge, Education, Resource, Discovery for You, embodies the spirit of this book. It's not just a journey through the world of AI; it's an invitation to embark on a lifelong adventure of learning, exploration, and constant evolution. As the field of AI progresses at an astonishing pace, so too must our understanding and engagement with it. The N.E.R.D.Y. Way encourages you to embrace this dynamic and ever-changing landscape as a catalyst for personal growth and societal advancement.

Think of it as an ongoing dialogue, a conversation between you and the world of AI, where curiosity is your compass and exploration is your guide. This journey is not about reaching a destination; it's about the continuous process of learning, adapting, and evolving alongside the ever-expanding frontiers of AI. Embrace the challenges and opportunities that come with this journey, for within them lies the potential to unlock your own capabilities and contribute to a future where technology empowers humanity.

The N.E.R.D.Y. Way is a mindset, a philosophy that encourages you to approach AI with a sense of wonder and a spirit of inquiry. It's about recognizing the profound impact AI is having on every aspect of our lives and acknowledging its potential to reshape our world. This mindset fosters a deep appreciation for the transformative power of AI while also recognizing the critical need for responsible development and deployment. It's about understanding the intricate workings of AI systems, their strengths, and limitations, and using this knowledge to make informed decisions about their use.

The N.E.R.D.Y. Way isn't just about acquiring knowledge; it's about applying it to create a better future. This journey is about using your understanding of AI to solve global challenges, foster collaboration between humans and machines, and shape a future where technology serves as a force for good. It's about embracing the responsibility that comes with this knowledge, recognizing that AI's future depends on our collective efforts.

As you delve deeper into the world of AI, remember that The N.E.R.D.Y. Way is not a solitary pursuit. It's a shared journey, one that connects you to a global community of researchers, developers, and enthusiasts who are working together to unlock the potential of AI. Engage with this community, share your insights, and contribute to the collective endeavor of shaping a brighter future.

Here are some practical ways to embrace The N.E.R.D.Y. Way:

- **Stay Curious:** Be a lifelong learner, constantly seeking new knowledge and understanding about AI. Explore new advancements, read articles, attend workshops, and engage in discussions with other enthusiasts.
- **Be an Active Participant:** Don't just passively observe the evolution of AI; actively participate in shaping its future. Engage in ethical discussions, advocate for responsible use, and contribute to research and development efforts.
- **Find Your Niche:** Identify areas of AI that resonate with your interests and passions, whether it's healthcare, finance, education, or something entirely different. Focus your learning and exploration on these areas, becoming an expert in your chosen field.
- **Collaborate and Share:** Engage with others in the AI community, sharing your insights, learning from their experiences, and working together to solve challenges and develop innovative solutions.

The N.E.R.D.Y. Way is a journey of discovery, a lifelong adventure in the ever-evolving world of AI. Embrace this mindset, stay curious, engage with the community, and contribute to shaping a future where technology empowers humanity for the benefit of all. It's not just about understanding AI; it's about becoming a part of it, a contributor to its future, and a champion for its responsible development and deployment. The future of AI is not a distant prospect; it's happening now, and it's up to us to shape it. The N.E.R.D.Y. Way is a call to action, a reminder that we all have a role to play in this journey, and every step we take, every question we ask, every idea we share, helps us move closer to a brighter future.

In the ever-evolving landscape of AI, embracing a lifelong journey of learning and exploration is not just desirable; it's essential. The N.E.R.D.Y. Way encourages you to approach this journey with a sense of wonder, curiosity, and a commitment to responsible innovation. As you delve deeper into the world of AI, remember that this isn't a solo expedition; it's a shared adventure. Connect with other enthusiasts, engage in dialogues, and contribute to the collective endeavor of shaping a future where AI serves humanity. The journey ahead is filled with both challenges and opportunities, and by embracing the N.E.R.D.Y. Way, you can unlock your own potential and contribute to a brighter future.

Think of the N.E.R.D.Y. Way as a compass, guiding you through the labyrinth of AI. It's not just about acquiring knowledge; it's about applying it, collaborating with others, and becoming an active participant in the ever-evolving landscape of AI. Embrace the spirit of discovery, stay curious, and contribute to building a future where AI empowers humanity.

For those who choose to embark on this journey, the rewards are boundless. You will gain a deeper understanding of the world around you, develop valuable skills, and contribute to a future where technology serves as a force for good. It's an invitation to join the conversation, to contribute to the dialogue, and to shape the future of AI for the benefit of all. The N.E.R.D.Y. Way is a testament to the power of learning, collaboration, and continuous exploration, a journey that will enrich your life and help build a better future for everyone.

The N.E.R.D.Y. Way isn't just about understanding AI; it's about becoming a part of its evolution, a contributor to its progress, and a champion for its responsible development and deployment. It's a reminder that the future of AI is not a distant prospect; it's happening now, and it's up to us to shape it. It's a call to action, a reminder that we all have a role to play in this journey, and every step we take, every question we ask, every idea we share, helps us move closer to a brighter future.

As you continue your journey, remember that the N.E.R.D.Y. Way is not just a concept; it's a mindset, a philosophy, and a call to action. It's a reminder that the future of AI is in our hands, and by embracing this mindset, we can unlock the potential of this powerful technology to create a better world for ourselves and future generations.

The Future of Now

The future is not some distant, hazy concept; it's unfolding right now, woven into the fabric of our daily lives. And at its heart lies artificial intelligence (AI), a technology with the potential to reshape our world in ways we're only beginning to grasp. This isn't a story of robots taking over; it's a story of collaboration, of humans and machines working together to overcome challenges and build a brighter future.

This journey into the world of AI begins with a simple question: How do we, as individuals, engage with this transformative technology? How do we take the first step towards understanding its power and shaping its future?

Imagine a world where AI helps us diagnose diseases with unprecedented accuracy, predict natural disasters to save lives, and personalize education to unlock each individual's potential. This is the future we can create, and it begins with each of us taking ownership of our role in this technological revolution.

The first step is curiosity. Embrace the wonder of AI. Explore the world of AI beyond the headlines and the hype. Ask questions, delve into the details, and don't be afraid to challenge your assumptions.

Next comes exploration. Dive into the vast ocean of information about AI. Explore online resources, documentaries, and articles. Experiment with AI tools and platforms. Start small, try a simple AI-powered game, or use a voice assistant to learn about a new topic. Every step you take, no matter how small, expands your understanding and builds your confidence.

Engage with the AI community. Connect with other enthusiasts, researchers, and developers. Participate in discussions, ask questions, and share your own insights. The power of community can be a powerful catalyst for learning and growth.

Remember, AI is a tool, and like any tool, its impact depends on how we use it. The future of AI is not predetermined; it's being shaped right now by the choices we make.

Let's be mindful of the ethical implications of AI. Consider the potential for bias in data and algorithms. Think about the impact of AI on employment and the need for reskilling and upskilling. Let's work together to ensure that AI is used for good, to empower humanity, and to create a world where everyone can thrive.

The future is not a destination; it's a journey. And it's a journey we embark on together, as individuals, as communities, and as a global society. The future is now, and the first step is ours to take.

This is the N.E.R.D.Y. way: kNowledge, Education, Resource, Discovery for You. It's a path of continuous learning and exploration, a commitment to understanding and shaping the future of AI. It's a journey that starts with a single step, a step that leads to a world where technology empowers humanity.

The journey begins with a simple question: What will you create?

Acknowledgments

This book would not have been possible without the invaluable contributions of many individuals. I am deeply grateful to the experts in Artificial Intelligence, Ethics, Psychology, and Sociology who collaborated with me on this project, sharing their knowledge, insights, and perspectives. Their guidance and expertise have shaped the book's content and deepened its understanding of the complex intersection of AI and human consciousness.

I am also indebted to my editor, [editor's name], for their meticulous attention to detail, insightful feedback, and unwavering support throughout the writing process. Their guidance has helped me to refine my ideas, clarify my arguments, and craft a more engaging and accessible narrative.

I would also like to thank the researchers, practitioners, and thought leaders who have generously shared their time, insights, and work with me. Their research and experiences have provided valuable context and inspiration for the book.

Finally, I am grateful to my family and friends for their unwavering encouragement and support, providing a much- needed source of inspiration and motivation during the long hours of writing.

Afterword

The creation of "The N.E.R.D.Y. Way: An Everyday Guide to AI" was a collaborative effort, and we are deeply grateful to everyone who contributed their expertise, insights, and unwavering support.

First and foremost, we would like to express our sincere gratitude to the 3CAT team for their meticulous research, insightful contributions, and dedication to crafting engaging and accessible content. Their collective expertise and passion were instrumental in bringing this book to life.

We extend our heartfelt thanks to the reviewers who provided valuable feedback and guidance throughout the writing process. Their thoughtful suggestions and constructive criticism helped shape the book into its final form.

We are also grateful to the individuals and organizations who generously shared their knowledge and experience, contributing to the depth and accuracy of the book. Their insights have enriched the content and provided valuable context for our readers.

Finally, we would like to thank our families and friends for their patience and understanding during the long hours spent writing and editing this book. Their unwavering support has been a source of inspiration and strength.

This appendix provides additional resources and information to complement the content discussed in the book.

APPENDIX & GLOSSARY

APPENDIX

A.1: AI Glossary

This glossary defines key terms and concepts related to artificial intelligence, providing readers with a comprehensive vocabulary for understanding the field.

A.2: AI Tools and Platforms

This section presents a curated list of popular AI tools and platforms, offering readers a starting point for exploring and experimenting with AI applications.

A.3: AI Datasets

This section provides a selection of publicly available datasets that can be used for AI research and development, empowering readers to delve deeper into practical AI applications.

A.4: AI Learning Resources

This section lists online courses, bootcamps, and other educational resources that can help individuals acquire AI skills and knowledge.

A.5: AI Community Links

This section provides links to online communities and forums where readers can connect with other AI enthusiasts and professionals, fostering a shared passion for learning and innovation.

Glossary

This glossary provides definitions for key terms and concepts discussed in the book, making it easier for readers to navigate the complex world of AI.

1. **Artificial Intelligence (AI):** The ability of a computer or machine to perform tasks that typically require human intelligence, such as learning, problem-solving, and decision-making.
2. **Machine Learning (ML):** A type of AI that enables computers to learn from data without explicit programming.
3. **Deep Learning (DL):** A subset of ML that uses artificial neural networks with multiple layers to process complex data patterns.
4. **Neural Network:** A computational model inspired by the structure and function of the human brain, consisting of interconnected nodes that process information.
5. **Supervised Learning:** A type of ML where algorithms are trained on labeled datasets, learning to predict outcomes based on input data.
6. **Unsupervised Learning:** A type of ML where algorithms are trained on unlabeled datasets, discovering hidden patterns and structures in the data.
7. **Reinforcement Learning:** A type of ML where algorithms learn through trial and error, optimizing their behavior based on feedback from the environment.
8. **Data:** The raw information that AI systems use to learn and make decisions.
9. **Algorithm:** A set of rules or instructions that AI systems use to process data and perform tasks.
10. **Bias:** Unwanted systematic errors or inequalities that can be introduced into AI systems due to biased data or algorithms.
11. **Ethics:** The moral principles and guidelines that govern the development and deployment of AI.
12. **Explainability:** The ability to understand and interpret the reasoning behind AI decisions, ensuring transparency and accountability.

References & Sources

This section provides a list of references and sources that were consulted in the writing of this book.

1. Russell, S. J., & Norvig, P. (2016). Artificial intelligence: A modern approach. Pearson Education.
2. Goodfellow, I., Bengio, Y., & Courville, A. (2016). Deep learning. MIT Press.
3. LeCun, Y., Bengio, Y., & Hinton, G. (2015). Deep learning. Nature, 521(7553), 436-444.
4. Minsky, M. (1967). Computation: Finite and infinite machines. Prentice-Hall.
5. McCarthy, J., Minsky, M. L., Rochester, N., & Shannon, C. E. (1955). A proposal for the Dartmouth summer research project on artificial intelligence.
6. Turing, A. M. (1950). Computing machinery and intelligence. Mind, 59(236), 433-460.
7. Floridi, L. (2014). The ethics of information technology: An introduction. Oxford University Press.
8. Bostrom, N. (2014). Superintelligence: Paths, dangers, strategies. Oxford University Press.
9. Calo, R. (2017). Artificial intelligence and the future of law. California Law Review, 105(5), 1157-1201.

About the Author
Dr. C.B. Howard, 3CAT

3CAT is a collective of professionals collaborating across various disciplines to offer innovative and practical solutions for individuals seeking to comprehend the effects of artificial intelligence (AI). We are committed to the dissemination of education and information, striving to enhance the lives of others. While knowledge is a powerful tool, its true potential is realized through its application.

At 3CAT, we acknowledge that everyone is unique. Consequently, we provide a diverse range of training and guidance materials tailored to accommodate different needs and learning preferences. Our publications cover a wide range of important topics, aiming to deepen understanding and knowledge in various areas of interest.

For every publication, 3CAT collaborates to conduct research, develop pertinent topics, create manuscripts, and oversee the publication process, to ensure the highest quality work possible.

The **N.E.R.D.Y.** WAY is an acronym for k**N**owledge, **E**ducation, **R**esource, **D**iscovery for **Y**ou.

The trademark for "The NERDY WAY" has been applied for and is currently pending.